# AFTER IRAQ:

# THE SEARCH FOR A SUSTAINABLE NATIONAL

# SECURITY STRATEGY

Colin S. Gray

January 2009

This manuscript was funded by the U.S. Army War College External Research Associates Program. Information on this program is available on our website, www.StrategicStudiesInstitute.army. mil, at the Publishing button.

\*\*\*\*\*

Comments pertaining to this report are invited and should be forwarded to: Director, Strategic Studies Institute, U.S. Army War College, 122 Forbes Ave, Carlisle, PA 17013-5244.

\*\*\*\*\*

All Strategic Studies Institute (SSI) publications are available on the SSI homepage for electronic dissemination. Hard copies of this report also may be ordered from our homepage. SSI's homepage address is: www.StrategicStudiesInstitute.army.mil.

\*\*\*\*\*

The Strategic Studies Institute publishes a monthly e-mail newsletter to update the national security community on the research of our analysts, recent and forthcoming publications, and upcoming conferences sponsored by the Institute. Each newsletter also provides a strategic commentary by one of our research analysts. If you are interested in receiving this newsletter, please subscribe on our homepage at www.StrategicStudiesInstitute. army.mil/newsletter/.

ISBN 1-58487-374-4

# FOREWORD

A sustainable national security strategy is feasible only when directed by a sustainable national security policy. In the absence of policy guidance, strategy has to be meaningless. The only policy that meets both the mandates of American culture and the challenges of the outside world is one that seeks to promote the necessary mission of guarding and advancing world order.

Dr. Colin Gray considers and rejects a policy that would encourage the emergence of a multipolar structure for global politics. He argues that multipolarity not only would fail to maintain order, it would also promote conflict among the inevitably rival great powers. In addition, he suggests that Americans culturally are not comfortable with balance-of-power politics and certainly would not choose to promote the return of such a system.

The monograph identifies the various "pieces of the puzzle" most relevant to national security strategy; surfaces the leading assumptions held by American policymakers and strategists; considers alternative national security policies; and specifies the necessary components of a sustainable national security strategy.

Dr. Gray concludes that America has much less choice over its policy and strategy than the public debate suggests. He warns that the country's dominant leadership role in global security certainly will be challenged before the century is old.

DOUGLAS C. LOVELACE, JR.
Director
Strategic Studies Institute

# BIOGRAPHICAL SKETCH OF THE AUTHOR

COLIN S. GRAY is Professor of International Politics and Strategic Studies at the University of Reading, England. He worked at the International Institute for Strategic Studies (London), and at Hudson Institute (Croton-on-Hudson, NY) before founding a defense-oriented think tank in the Washington, DC, area, the National Institute for Public Policy. Dr. Gray served for 5 years in the Reagan administration on the President's General Advisory Committee on Arms Control and Disarmament. He has served as an adviser to both the U.S. and British governments (he has dual citizenship). His government work has included studies of nuclear strategy, arms control, maritime strategy, space strategy, and the use of special forces. Dr. Gray has written 22 books, including *The Sheriff: America's Defense of the New World Order* (University Press of Kentucky, 2004), and *Another Bloody Century: Future Warfare* (Weidenfeld and Nicolson, 2005). In 2006 he published *Strategy and History: Essays on Theory and Practice* (Routledge). His most recent books are *War, Peace, and International Relations: An Introduction to Strategic History* (Routledge, 2007; Potomac Books, 2009), and *National Security Dilemmas: Challenges and Opportunities* (Potomac Books, 2009). His next book, recently completed, is *The Strategy Bridge: Theory for Practice*. Dr. Gray is a graduate of the Universities of Manchester and Oxford.

# SUMMARY

What should be the U.S. national security strategy after Iraq? An answer cannot be given unless a logically and politically prior question is posed: "What should be the purpose and character of a sustainable U.S. national security policy after Iraq?" Thus to answer the first question, one has to identify both the policy that strategy must serve as well as the components of that strategy.

Unfortunately for the convenience and self-confidence of defense planners, although the 21st century presents no great difficulty to America over its choice of national security policy, the selection of a suitable strategy is a far more difficult task. The challenge is cultural and material. U.S. national culture favors both a somewhat disengaged stance towards the world beyond North America, as well as the active promotion of such leading American values as freedom, democracy, and open markets. On the material side, the country faces an exceptionally wide range of actual and potential threats to its vital interests by historical standards. On the one hand, there are nonstate terrorists and other insurgents of an Islamist Jihadist persuasion who could threaten the stability of the global economy by menacing commercial access to oil, and who may well acquire a few weapons of mass destruction (WMD). On the other hand, the new century appears certain to see the rise of some current regional powers to a yet greater category, China and India specifically. When we add in current uncertainty about the future course of Russian policy, the European Union as a possible super state, as well as the future roles of Japan and Iran, it becomes readily apparent that the years ahead offer few certainties regarding U.S. threat priorities.

U.S. national security policy can be sustainable only if it meets domestic cultural standards as well as the externally-based demands to which American leaders must respond out of a prudent concern for protection of national interests. Therefore, it is necessary to appreciate the domain of necessity or nearly such, both domestic and foreign. U.S. policy and strategy have to satisfy in two markets, at home and abroad.

Scholars debate whether American culture, or a supposedly "objective" foreign material reality, ultimately commands policy and strategy. The debate is foolish. In practice, Americans attempt what they are able, as they perceive and interpret international conditions, in a manner that cannot help reflecting American cultural influence.

In order to identify a sustainable national security strategy, it is essential to recognize, and take due account of, the whole hierarchy of relevant ideas and behavior. To specify, the strategy in question here is conditioned by the following factors:

- Perceived state of the world
- U.S. role in the world
- Policy
- National security strategy
- Military strategy
- Military forces.

With which major working assumptions are American policymakers and strategists forearmed? Individuals undoubtedly will dissent in some detail from any particular listing, but the following is a plausible summary of the principal assumptions that equip the senior ranks of America's national security policymaking community:

- *War is endemic in the human condition.* Though it is culturally American to be generically hopeful, U.S. defense planners cannot, and do not, assume that the 21st century will witness the end of war.

- *Warfare will both evolve and appear in several forms.* Future hostilities will be regular and irregular; among states as well as states and nonstate political entities. Radically new technologies will impact warfare of all kinds.
- *Global order is a meaningful concept; such order has to be policed by someone or something.* Theories of order promotion abound; most are illusory. The alternative to order is disorder, and the spectrum from tolerable order to intolerable disorder is not usually smoothly linear; it is marked eccentrically by tipping points. Also, order–disorder is a condition that applies across several dimensions of global affairs, for example economic-financial as well as military-strategic. As a general rule, the path to ruin will be unmistakably apparent only in hindsight.
- *War entails warfare, and warfare always is about fighting.* America's armed forces must excel in warfare of all kinds, regular and irregular. This is not to say, however, that the two are of equal importance; they are not. The country should continue to accord top priority to its military prowess in interstate warfare, even if that prospective combat is anticipated to be significantly asymmetrical.
- *New first-class competitors/enemies will emerge (indeed, are emerging already).* The relatively few years since 1991 have been remarkable in world politics for the absence of a state or coalition able to balance the U.S. superpower. They have not been remarkable as heralding a revolution in

the functioning of that politics. Of recent years, no one has been strong enough to constrain the United States. Such a power would, and predictably will, attract follower-states in due course. World order in the 21st century will not be overseen by an executive committee of the rather virtual world community, led by an ever comfortably dominant America. If that benign arrangement truly were in the offing, it would be manifest in the behavior and norms of the United Nations Security Council. It is not. Rising states such as China and India are on a collision course with each other and possibly with the United States. Emerging regional great powers, let alone new super states, will accept U.S. leadership in some security matters only if that leadership serves their national interest in helping to offset the strength of regional rivals. The structure of relative power and influence, by region and globally, is dynamic. If a state, even a superpower, is not rising it is very likely to be falling. History has not come to a happy conclusion with American dominance.

- *Surprise happens.* There are unknowns, and even "unknown unknowns," in America's future, as a recent Secretary of Defense observed with eloquent opaqueness. A sustainable U.S. national security strategy needs to be surprise-proofed in the sense of being robust when confronted with the unexpected. Given the range of radical new technologies with potential military applications that should mature in the 21st century, and given a predictable context of international rivalry or worse, U.S. defense planners are obliged to favor flexibility and adaptability.

U.S. policy to provide purpose and political guidance to U.S. strategy in the future is usefully approachable by identifying four fairly distinctive alternative American roles in the world. These are readily characterized as follows:

1. Hegemon-leader for global guardianship
2. Anti-hegemonial offshore balancer and spoiler
3. Disengaged lone wolf
4. Moderate competitor and partner in a multipolar world.

Of the four nominal choices, only the first is truly practicable at present and in the near-term future. The partnership in multipolarity, an idea that appeals to many scholars, is flawed in that the non-American "poles" are not yet ready for prime time. Furthermore, even if this were not the case, a genuinely multipolar world would be prone to great power wars. The rich strategic history of multipolarity is far from encouraging. The role of "disengaged lone wolf" simply could not work. The United States is engaged in world affairs by economic, environmental, and hence political and potentially strategic, globalization. To be disengaged would be to decline to protect one's vital interests. Moreover, America's national culture, though marked by a longing for disengagement, also strongly favors political missionary behavior. This latter value rises and falls irregularly, but it always rises again.

The United States could try to effect a transition from its current on-shore Eurasian strategy of forward deployment, to an off-shore posture keyed to a policy role as "spoiler" of potential grand continental coalitions. As maritime-air-space balancer of large Eurasian menaces, the United States would both retain its political discretion over belligerency and favor its national strength in the higher technology features of its armed forces. The problem is that this off-shore role would not suffice to defend the national interest. The country would not be trusted, since it would eschew the firm commitments that require local presence. As much to the point, U.S. influence would be certain to diminish as a consequence of a process of withdrawal, no matter how impressive the reach of America's weapons through the several geographies of the great "commons."

Almost by default, the United States should choose, perhaps simply accept, the role of hegemon-leader for a world order that serves both its own most vital interests as well as those of a clear majority of members of the world community, such as it is. Contrary to the sense of much of the contemporary debate, Americans have no prudent alternative other than to play the hegemonic role. But for the role to be sustainable, it has to rest upon the formal or tacit consent of other societies. Only with such consent will America be able to exercise a national security strategy geared successfully to the ordering duty.

What are the components of a sustainable national security strategy, given the necessity for a guiding policy whose overarching purpose is to protect the national interest by defending world order globally? Such a strategy must be refined and adapted to specific cases, but these are its generic constituents:

1. *Control of the global commons* (sea, air, space, cyberspace), when and where it is strategically essential.

2. *The ability to dissuade, deter, defeat, or at least largely neutralize any state, coalition of states, or nonstate political actor, that threatens regional or global order.*

3. *Adaptable and flexible strategy, operations, tactics, logistics, and forces.* Future wars and warfare will occur all along the spectrum of regularity-irregularity. Asymmetry will be the norm, not the exception, even in regular conventional hostilities.

4. *Continuing supremacy in regular conventional combat.* Prediction of a strategic future that will be wholly irregular is almost certainly a considerable exaggeration.

5. *Competence in counterinsurgency (COIN) and counterterror (CT).* These activities should not dominate American defense preparation and action, but they comprise necessary military, inter alia, core competencies.

6. *Excellence in raiding,* thus exploiting the leverage of America's global reach.

7. *First-rate strategic theory and strategic and military doctrine.* Ideas are more important than machines, up to a point at least.

8. *A national security, or grand, strategy worthy of the name,* in which military strategy can be suitably "nested."

9. *Policy choices and tactical military habits that do not offend American culture.*

10. *A fully functioning "strategy bridge"* that binds together, adaptably, the realms of policy and military behavior.

Our analysis concludes by identifying five far-reaching points of great concern. First, the preferred option, truly the necessary choice, for the United States in the world, here called "hegemony-primacy-light," is a policy condition, not a strategy. Americans have proved vulnerable to the temptation to leap from policy selection to military operations, largely neglecting the essential levels of grand strategy and military strategy.

Second, a definite strategy needs a definite enemy. This reality all but encourages oversimplification. America can wage war against al-Qaeda, but not against "terror." Because the identity of most of the country's future enemies is uncertain, it must suffice to ensure that the "components" from which definite strategies would be constructed are always ready for play when the strategy coach calls on them to perform.

Third, the United States needs to beware of false alternatives for its policy and strategy. In defense of its national interests, the country has no prudent alternatives other than to play the hegemonic role for as long as it is able. Similarly, there is no sensible alternative to some on-shore entanglements in Eurasia, though assuredly Americans should strive to succeed more by raiding than by intervening in, and occupying, alien territory. There are and will be cases when American boots must grind local dust. However, the U.S. hegemon should seek to tread as lightly as the mission permits, lest its effort triggers a self-defeating "blowback" from an outraged and formerly neutral local population. Unfortunately, more often than not strategic and political effectiveness are much enhanced when the military has overwhelming force and applies it.

Fourth, belatedly Washington has learned what a handful of scholars, not to mention the World War II generation of policymakers, knew, i.e., that culture as a force must never be underestimated. Understanding of one's own culture as well as the culture of others can make the difference between success and failure in policy, strategy, operations, and tactics.

Fifth, America must understand that its dominant role in many dimensions of world affairs increasingly will be challenged by those whose interests, anxieties, and honor are challenged by the U.S. hegemony. No matter how gingerly this hegemony is manifested in U.S. behavior, it will be resented and opposed.

# AFTER IRAQ:
# THE SEARCH FOR A SUSTAINABLE NATIONAL SECURITY STRATEGY

If American hegemony is the answer, what was the question?

Anonymous

Thus it is said that one who knows the enemy and knows himself will not be endangered in a hundred engagements. One who does not know the enemy but knows himself will sometimes be victorious, sometimes meet with defeat. One who knows neither the enemy nor himself will invariably be defeated in every engagement.

Sun-tzu, ca. 400BC, 1994[1]

In the 5th century, it was dawning on the Roman world, especially Constantinople, that theirs was but one state among many: a perception which contrasted with the 4th-century view that Rome comprised the entire civilized world.

Ross Laidlaw, 2007[2]

## Introduction: Home and Abroad.

Strategy and policy are not synonymous. However, a sustainable strategy can serve only a sustainable policy. If the latter oscillates, the former becomes impractical. This monograph targets primarily the national, or grand, strategic level of analysis, but it cannot ignore the challenge of ascertaining and sustaining a coherent national security policy. Carelessly or for stylistic variety, many politicians, analysts, and commentators employ the terms policy and strategy interchangeably.[3] This malpractice does not scar these pages. The distinction matters crucially and needs to be maintained rigorously. Policy sets goals, indeed may well change goals, while strategy is always instrumental. In the absence of a reasonably stable policy, strategy becomes literally meaningless; it must lack political direction.

The first epigraph above highlights both the core of the contemporary debate about America's place in the world, and reminds people of the need to be clear about the underlying purpose behind a sweeping policy goal. The discussion that follows addresses both the national and the international levels of analysis. It probes the probable structure and functioning of global politics as well as America's role. This is not an exercise in the academic study of International Relations, but it cannot be denied that it must bear directly, and draw upon, a major debate within the international community of scholars.[4] Specifically, scholars of International Relations are debating energetically the respective and relative influence of the material structure of the international system of states (very largely), as opposed to the potency of domestic cultures (national, strategic, and military-institutional).[5] For once, academics are focusing on an issue area that has immense meaning for U.S. policy and strategy. In fact, widespread expert misunderstanding of the relationship between what one can summarize for convenience as power and culture is misleading much of the current public debate on the subject of this monograph. The two should not be presented as rivals; in practice both are players.

The second epigraph is essential, even though it is almost tediously familiar. It points to the heart of what must be the argument here. Specifically, Americans have to know themselves as foreign policy players. More to the point, they should recognize the uniqueness and content of their collective national culture. A large fraction of public debate about U.S. foreign policy and national security strategy in the 21st century is all but irrelevant, because it refers to imaginary Americans. To state the twin basics of this subject: U.S. national security strategy, and the policy it serves, has to be a response to the international structure of power, as strategy is shaped, driven, or fine-tuned by U.S. national culture. To be truly blunt, Americans are what they are and believe what they believe. Their deepest values, assumptions, attitudes, and even behavioral habits are the products of the national historical experience as it has been, and is being, interpreted and reinterpreted. A national policy or strategy that is not sustainable when challenged by the values of domestic culture must fail.[6] For example, the United States does not "do" balance of power politics or multipolar systems of order, at least it has not yet. Moreover, it shows no official or popular, as contrasted with scholarly, inclination to shift seamlessly into such a novel and culturally unwelcome groove.

The cultural claim registered immediately above is not just a minor academic point. Rather, it amounts to the statement that unless one takes generous account of American domestic national culture, analysis of, and recommendations for, U.S. policy and strategy are near certain to be irrelevant. This is why so much of the current still-burgeoning controversy over the future of American external behavior is by and large off the mark. The problem is not limited to the fact that many people do not take proper account of American ideology. In addition, even when they do note the unhelpful or complicating factor of ideas, they choose to discount it.[7]

To illustrate the huge scale of the problem that underlies this enquiry, consider the fundamental challenge to the United States in Afghanistan and Iraq. In both cases, Americans are attempting what may well prove to be a mission impossible. Neither "country" — or seriously "undergoverned space," to coin a phrase — has given convincing evidence of being ripe for transformation into a market democracy. The difficulty is that Afghans, Iraqis, and Americans cannot help being who they are, with the beliefs that they have inherited and nursed. It is a matter of identity. By and large, Americans are not cynical exploiters, while Afghans and Iraqis are not generally ignorant and cowed, though there is certainly plenty of that to be found. Each culture, with its subcultures, is the product of its geography and history and will change only slowly. As a prominent British historian has written recently: "The view that American ideology and technology would transcend Iraqi political culture was mistaken."[8] Iraq can be transformed only within its own complex cultural parameters, not in defiance of them, and then only by Iraqis.

Intrinsically, Americans have no free choice in deciding whether or not to stand for, and frequently try to advance, their essentially liberal notions of democracy and of prosperity through free trade. It is not a question of choice. As claimed already, democracy and freedom through the benefits of a prosperous open economy are central to the American identity. This credo and these values can be ignored in practice on occasion, thereby attracting well-merited charges of hypocrisy. But in its prevailing direction, U.S. foreign policy and national security strategy are certain to be influenced by the culturally-driven desire to improve the world. Such is the enduring significance of culture. However, this is not the whole story by any means. What happens when U.S. policy and strategy are frustrated, as has been the case in Afghanistan and Iraq? And how does the United States react when it anticipates a global future less hospitable to U.S. leadership than has obtained in recent years? This is the fundamental dynamic context addressed here. How hard should Americans try to remain clearly the Number One power? The United States requires a national security strategy and policy sustainable in what is sure to be a future quite hostile to American values and assumptions.

The long list of U.S. problems in Afghanistan and Iraq should not be misinterpreted. It would be a mistake to conclude that: (1) the United States should cease to act hegemonically; (2) U.S. values (i.e., culture) are flawed, for Americans and some others; (3) the U.S. armed forces have been demonstrably incompetent. A more sensible interpretation of events would be the following: (1) the United States is the only candidate for contemporary hegemon, and world order needs a hegemon willing and able to serve as world policeman, even one that makes some policy errors[9]; (2) in major respects U.S. culture is highly attractive, which is fortunate since it is not easily alterable, but it does need to be advertised and applied with care and restraint abroad; (3) Americans have become very competent at warfighting, but that prowess has not extended across the whole of the conflict spectrum. In common with all great powers in the past, the United States has to learn to cope with occasional policy failure. Failure through human error or sheer incompetence, friction, and bad luck should not be mistaken for precipitate decline. Too many commentators today are proclaiming the end of American hegemony. It is true that there are visible trends hostile to U.S. hegemony, the well-announced "rise of " China and India, and one day, just possibly, the EU/Europe, and even a long-delayed Japan and Brazil. But for the time being and for many years to come, the United States will be the hegemon. This is to say that it will be the global leader, certainly the most important player, in any matter of grave significance for international security. This will be what one might call a default reality. It is, and will be, a consequence of conscious American choice and effort. Also, U.S. leadership, notwithstanding the exception of its behavior towards Iraq, will rest upon a base provided by broad global consent, albeit not always of an enthusiastic kind.

Despite the discretion theoretically permitted by the virtual geographical insularity of the U.S. homeland, American policy and grand strategy have been unmistakably stable when historically viewed. Truly great debates on America's place and role in the outside world, as well as on its high policy towards that world, have been few and far between. The current ferment of ideas and assertions is most unusual. In fact, not since the late 1940s has there been a public debate on U.S. foreign policy and national security policy at all comparable to the present controversy.

As for national security strategy, for the nearest historical precedent for the depth of contemporary arguments one has to look back to the first Eisenhower administration (1953-57), when the country struggled to come to terms with nuclear realities. In both foreign policy and military strategy, the United States settled upon what proved to be sustainable pillars. Americans determined to lead and be the principal material contributor to a global anti-Communist alliance. That ideologically and economically sustainable decision was undergirded by the decision to place heavy reliance upon nuclear deterrence. Washington realized swiftly that there was little it could do, or was prepared to attempt, to prevent such deterrence from becoming inconveniently mutual with respect to the Communist bloc. The basic thrust of U.S. policy and strategy was not to alter for 40 years, through no fewer than nine presidencies. This is not to endorse the strategic choice that was made, but simply to note the longevity of its authority.

If one looks to the *longue durée,* one finds that there has been a distinctive geopolitical, hence geostrategic, pattern to U.S. national security behavior.[10] Those scholars who point to an oscillation in American policy between expansion and withdrawal, relative introversion and extroversion, are substantially correct. Ideologically, which is to say culturally, Americans desire both to remake the world into a facsimile of their own New World, and to effect that monumental task at distinctly limited cost.[11] This cultural conflict lies at the heart of today's American national security debate. From the time of America's first emergence as a player of world politics, which one can date generously to the defeat of Spain in 1899, until today, the country has intervened with massive force on the world stage on four occasions: 1917-18; 1941-45; 1946-91; and 2001-present. In each case, the United States stepped in violently, twice by irresistible invitation (1941 and 2001), to resolve problems of Eurasian security.

In each of the first three periods, the United States stayed the course until the job was done, either militarily (1918, 1945) or politically (1991). However, September 11, 2001 (9/11) was different. The announcement of a "long war," a "global war on terror" (GWOT)—both terms have now lost most of

7

their official favor—has come to appear as necessary in broad policy principle as it may be misconceived in some contemporary practice.[12] The fact that 9/11 was directed at Americans at home compensates somewhat for the historical reality that terrorism is in the lesser category of threats to national security. Not many years ago the U.S. defense community was anticipating the possibility of the country suffering tens of millions of casualties, at the least, should there be a breakdown in the stability of mutual deterrence. Even an al-Qaeda affiliate improbably armed with, and able to deploy, one or two nuclear devices could not begin to pose a menace comparable in scale to the erstwhile Soviet danger. Terrorism, especially terrorism with weapons of mass destruction (WMD), may be the "threat of the week," but it is easy to exaggerate its potency.

As we have seen, the national culture commands opposing impulses: on the one hand, to democratize/Americanize the world; on the other, to stay at home in the comfort and now only relative security of North America. But despite those domestic realities, Americans have been quite steady in their approach to international security. One can argue that the United States declined to accept its responsibility as a newly minted very great power in 1919 and the subsequent two decades. However, it is well to recall that in those years France and Britain were still regarded widely as great powers and, de facto, were behaving, perhaps misbehaving, on behalf of the United States, geostrategically.[13] In East Asia the United States eventually, by 1940, did accept the leadership of an anti-Japanese coalition. Neither deterrence nor coercion short of force could dissuade Japan from its pursuit of continental empire in China, but Washington was firmly committed to resisting such Japanese imperialism.

When Britain and France were demoted by the course of strategic history from the first rank of great powers, the United States did not delay long before it picked up the fallen flag for Western values and geopolitical interests. But since 1946, or 1941 if preferred, the United States has sustained resolutely as much of an anti-hegemonic policy towards Eurasia as it believed was needed.[14] With the fall of the Soviet imperium, however, Washington was left by default as global hegemon, or world leader, the dominant power. Triggered by 9/11, the United States chose to become the hegemon with a predominant purpose, to conduct a GWOT. Whether the "long war" against terrorists is sustainable as the centerpiece of U.S. national security strategy, there are grounds to doubt. The principal reason for skepticism is not so much uncertainty over the persistence of violent Islamism. Rather, doubts accrue as to the prospect of a recognizable victory. Furthermore, other global developments are likely to reduce the relative significance of the terrorist menace.

When considered over the longer term, as in this monograph, U.S. foreign policy, national security policy, and strategy must reconcile the demands of a domestic culture that can have dysfunctional consequences abroad, with the objective circumstances of the outside world. It is almost entirely useless for American or other scholars to write books and articles urging a U.S. policy that affronts American culture. The beginning of wisdom has to be with Sun-tzu's dictum on the necessity for knowledge of the enemy and of oneself. To be sustainable, American policy and strategy must be broadly compatible with American values. Perhaps not all American values, and not all of the time. But any policy vision that is plainly un-

American is certain to fail at home eventually. Foreign policy is born at home and has to succeed there if it is to succeed abroad.

The current debate to which this monograph relates is replete with arguments about anticipated features of the 21st century that will prove desperately challenging to American national culture. It may well be that this century will see a return of multipolar balance-of-power politics on a global scale. But when one considers this possibility, even probability, one needs to remember that American culture wants to reject what it regards as the cynical balance-of-power politics of expediency. Americans believe it is a mission of their unique country to improve the world. If thwarted in this noble, even (in the opinion of many) divine, mission, they are likely to insist that the country withdraw, adopting a minimalist foreign policy. Controversialist Christopher Layne speaks for many Americans when he writes: "Precisely because of its power and geography, there is very little the United States needs to do in the world in order to be secure."[15] This is not a majority opinion at present, but it does express a powerful enduring current in American culture.

Any and all discussion of a sustainable U.S. national security strategy must be at least as attentive to the persisting realities of American culture as it is to the constraints and opportunities of the outside world. In addition, many scholars and even some official planners are apt to neglect the potent roles that can be played by eccentric personal preference, incompetence, error, pure accident, and unavoidable bad luck. The realm of national security strategy is far from friction free.[16]

The body of this work opens with an explanation of the structure of the subject of national security strategy; it then attempts to peer into the future to identify assumptions that should be robust, albeit with caveats attached. Next, the discussion specifies the most desirable American role in the world of the 21st century. From the American role, the analysis moves on to consider the most appropriate strategy. The monograph closes with observations and recommendations on national security strategy.

**The Strategic Challenge.**

Because of the inherent complexity of our subject, it is most important to appreciate both the whole structure that is relevant and its parts, as well as how the structure of strategy should function. National security strategy can make no sense if approached in isolation.[17] It is not self-referential. It must express and serve a national security policy. In addition, it has to be implemented by agencies, military and civilian, whose capabilities roughly match the authoritative goals. The strategic challenge in the title of this section is the difficulty of keeping ways, means, and ends approximately in balance so that they are mutually supportive.[18] This task is extraordinarily difficult to accomplish. The principal source of difficulty may repose with policy goals that overreach or underreach; with purposeful strategy that does not advance policy, or even the complete absence of such strategy; or with military and other means that are excessive or inadequate. Michael Howard offers the counterintuitive judgment that "the strategy adopted is always more likely to be dictated rather by the availability of means than by the nature of the ends."[19] Although this view has major merit, it can mislead. While it is true to claim that as a general rule a government "makes war, not as one would like

11

to, but as one must,"[20] it is also the case that the United States often has suffered from a strategy deficit.[21] The whole structure of our subject has the following components:

1. Culture (e.g., values, vision)
2. U.S. role in the world
3. State of the world, international environment
4. National security policy
5. National security strategy
6. Military strategy
7. Military forces.

American *national culture* is always liable to contribute significantly to external policy. Culture expresses the nation's dominant values and its vision of how the world ought to be and how the country should relate to that world. Just as it would be absurd to interpret American history without regard to the ideas and beliefs that have shaped, even ruled, American minds, so it would be unsound to treat the future of American national security policy and strategy without accounting for the potential influence of culture. Americans do not and will not behave abroad strictly as rational actors coldly assessing their national interest in material terms. The United States assuredly will seek to overbalance possibly menacing physical power. But Washington will assess, calculate, and behave for purposes and in terms that are ideational as well as material-structural. For example, the United States will strive not merely to keep the People's Republic of China (PRC) materially subordinate with reference to the power balance. In addition, it will strive to "improve" China as well as America's global trading partners and dependents. Beyond the national culture expressed in the ideals of liberty, freedom, democracy, and open markets, American culture has strategic and military-institutional branches. There is an "American way of war" that reflects the national geography, history, and ideology.[22] However, culture, though important, does not alone determine policy and strategy. Objective material realities are an ever possible source of constraint on national preference, as are the surprise effects of unexpected happenings. Culture is important, but it is not all-important.

America's *role in the world* is much more the product of cultural choice than is usual for most countries.[23] One can plead strategic necessity for many of the country's wars: for a supposedly peace-loving democracy, there have been many such.[24] But on close inspection, the national geography truly donated a large measure of policy discretion to America's statesmen. Americans now are more than comfortable with the idea that the United States is Number One. The implications of unipolarity after 1991 (or 1989, with the collapse of the Soviet imperium) are not always plain, but the American public has accustomed itself to the idea of primacy, even hegemony in the sense of global leadership.

To be the global hegemon is a role that only the United States can play, whether it performs well or poorly. However, the country is not an ideologically disinterested, effectively neutral, guardian of world order. This sheriff aspires to extend the domain of its interpretation of good law, not merely to enforce it in areas already civilized.[25] Very occasionally, Americans debate the ways and means to implement their role in the world, but the ends are constant and nonnegotiable. Historically speaking, there have been few exceptions among American statesmen to those who have signed on in the Golden Book for freedom and democracy.

One can always find a stand-out, a true pragmatist untroubled by the manifest desirability of operating a value-free foreign policy. Richard M. Nixon and his eminence grise, Henry Kissinger, spring to mind.[26] Nonetheless, one would find it difficult to people a dinner party of modest size with American leaders from all periods who were wholehearted practitioners of that game of nations, *Realpolitik*. America's role in the world should, not must, accommodate irresistible external pressures and elements, but it will do so in an American way. This way is not a single-lane highway. Nonetheless, no matter how particular American leaders play their hand in global politics, their style will reflect the national culture which they share.

American culture has to function, even bow to, the external context. The dynamic *state of the world*, the international environment as scholars have come to call it, is a complex objective reality that Americans can do little to alter. This is not to deny that the United States is by far the most influential player of global politics. Furthermore, it is not to forget that the country periodically is inclined to exaggerate its potential to reshape that reality to its own preferred image. The recent, and just about still current, U.S. (actually Anglo-American) crusade for democracy is a classic expression of this American tendency to overreach. Whether or not there is a valid connection between the democratization of formerly politically pagan lands and progress in the GWOT is really moot. The world cannot be democratized by American power and influence and neither can it be converted by American domestic example. As a general rule, a stable democracy has to be almost wholly a domestic growth. Appreciation of that aspect of the contemporary state of the world is not much in dispute among scholars.

The world political system is still unipolar, and it should remain so for some years to come.[27] Nonetheless, there is widespread agreement that the United States is in relative decline, as other, currently regional, powers, increase their individual strength vis-à-vis the U.S. hegemon. Since 2003 in particular, which saw the Anglo-American invasion of Iraq on March 17, some regional great powers, actual and aspiring, have made a habit of collaborating to try to clip the American eagle's wings.[28] This political development was inevitable. The only questions were, and remain, how soon would a coalition, probably only a loose one at first, emerge to challenge U.S. hegemonism, how effective would it prove to be, and how would the United States react? These are the questions that underlie contemporary domestic America and foreign debate. Many scholars and journalists are fond of identifying the course of current events as the turning of a historical corner. The metaphor is popular and benefits from an absence of temporal perspective. At present, one can suggest the global political system is still unipolar, broadly if unevenly policed by American culture, and, if needs be, by American threats or the actual use of military force. But America's "unipolar moment" allegedly is either passing or already has receded into history. It was foreshortened by the muscular errors that produced imperial overstretch in Afghanistan and Iraq, so the narrative runs.[29] In place of American hegemony—a complex reality that requires closer attention than it is usually granted, as the ever perceptive Jeremy Black reminds us[30]—a new era of multipolarity allegedly is dawning. This may be a sound prediction. Indeed, in the long run it is all but certain to be correct. But it is by no means self-evident that America's "moment" of unshared, unbalanced, strategic preponderance must vanish any time soon. There is widespread agreement, therefore, among the U.S. commentariat that multipolarity is the future. However, whether that future is near-term one ought to doubt. Furthermore, few of the prophets of multipolarity appear to understand the problems with the condition they espouse.

The state of the world, the context wherein the United States must locate and exercise its role, is flush with troubles, actual and for once fairly reliably predictable. A sustainable U.S. national security strategy will need to be effective in coping with the following leading threats to American and global well-being, presented here in descending order of probable significance:

1. Return of great power conflict (i.e., multipolarity).

2. Climate change: resource shortages — water, food, energy.

3. Overpopulation, illegal mass migration, policy pressures in overpopulated countries, pandemics.

4. Globalization: economic, cultural, political, military — very uneven development and prosperity.

5. Nuclear proliferation and regional nuclear wars.

6. "Islamist" terrorism.

These are not alternatives. They will occur in bunches, simultaneously and interdependently in some cases. Obviously, climate change, overpopulation, and uneven development comprise a witch's brew of menaces to international order. Scholars will differ over an item or two among the six offered, certainly in their suggested prioritization. But overall, these six sources of trouble are postulated with high confidence. It will be in the context provided by these dynamic difficulties that Americans will seek to be strategically effective in a sustainable way.

Next, it is mandatory that a clear distinction be maintained between *national security policy* and *national security strategy*. At some risk of banality, this analysis insists upon crystal clarity in their relationship, even though there needs to be a continuous discourse between them. Civilian policymakers should influence generals and vice versa. But that dialogue, appropriately termed unequal by Eliot Cohen because of the necessity for civilian control, should not transform politicians functionally into generals nor generals into politicians.[31] A national security strategy must be a joint civil-military product. It should be created, exercised, and, when essential, revised, with vital inputs from both civilians and soldiers.[32] Nonetheless, national security strategy can always only be instrumental. If one seeks to understand what the strategy is supposed to achieve, one must lift one's gaze and examine policy. This is where political intentions have to be specified.

In practice, culture or material temptation sometimes drives policy and strategy without the two engaging in honest and realistic dialogue. Policy may specify goals that are chosen for desirability, with scant attention paid to feasibility. For example, U.S. policy has sought to democratize Iraq and trigger a benign democratic revolution throughout the realm of Islam. It is a serious mistake to confuse national security policy, let alone national security strategy, with foreign policy. National security, or grand, strategy, refers in all definitions to the potential or actual orchestration of any and every national asset for purposes selected by national security policy. But those purposes need to entail some risk of war.[33] Grand strategy can be pursued in time of peace as well as war, but it is important to use the concept only when the military dimension is prominent and the use

17

of force is a distinct possibility, if not probability. In the same way that strategic studies must not be subsumed into an overly broad, all-dangers, security studies, so national security strategy has to retain a strong military flavor, despite its breadth of domain.[34]

Under the umbrella of national security strategy lies *military strategy*. Confusion of the two is commonplace. Although war most essentially entails fighting, as Carl von Clausewitz insists, not every exercise of national security strategy requires warfare.[35] Adroit diplomacy or cunningly applied economic coercion may remove need for the spilling of blood. However, since national security strategy has the military element at its core, it must follow that military strategy is nearly always critical to the success of policy. If the United States chooses and conducts military strategy incompetently to the point of battlefield defeat on a theater-wide scale, it is unlikely to be possible to find adequate compensation through the skillful employment of other agencies of national power and influence. Once committed to a conflict, military force has a way of mattering more than anything else. Even though fighting is not always potentially the most effective source of strategic effect, if one loses in combat the fighting will assume the pole position in relative significance.

Most typically, the regular side in irregular warfare cannot win the war as a whole militarily, but paradoxically, even ironically, it can be defeated by failure in combat. In 1964, Bernard B. Fall expressed the condition thus:

> [G]uerrilla warfare is nothing but a tactical appendage of a far vaster political contest and . . . no matter how expertly it is fought by competent and dedicated professionals, it cannot possibly make up for the absence of a political rationale.[36]

In both Iraq and Afghanistan today, growing U.S. competence in counterinsurgency (COIN) and counterterror (CT) has not until recently been married to a political rationale sufficiently favored by local power brokers. As a result, it is uncertain as to whether U.S. COIN efforts will produce the lasting political effects sought by Washington.

In 1954, the defeat of the 17 elite battalions (only 10 fought any one time) of the French Colonial Army at Dien Bien Phu had conclusive political consequences, albeit not ones that fully satisfied the Vietnamese.[37] Ho Chi Minh was bullied by China and Russia into tolerating the temporary creation of a South Vietnam. For the exception to the rule that defeat in battle is fatal, it is historically accurate to note that although French colonial forces won the fighting in Algeria, France lost the war.[38] For further illustration, it can be persuasively argued that the United States defeated the Viet Cong and the North Vietnamese Army (NVA) in resisting the Tet Offensive in 1968, as well as in subsequent operations, yet still lost the war.

This monograph recognizes the sovereignty of politics over warfare and endorses the view that there are some conflicts that cannot be concluded successfully by military means. But we also wish to contradict the all too prevalent notion that actual fighting is only of secondary importance. The view taken here is that the primacy of politics, indeed of culture, does not mean that tactical military outcomes are of little significance. To stumble into that opinion is to overreach with the sound argument that military success does not necessarily translate into victory in a war overall.[39]

The final piece of the puzzle tackled here is the *armed forces*: soldiers, their morale, institutions, doctrines, training, tactical skills, equipment, and combat effectiveness or fighting power. Military strategy should change only at a pace consistent with actual military prowess. If the armed forces cannot perform adequately at their core or defining activity of fighting, then military strategy, national security strategy, and policy will be frustrated. The soldiers of the Third Reich could not defeat the soldiers of Soviet Russia. German military strategy faltered and collapsed in the face of too much distance, too large an enemy, and repeated logistical disasters and other systemic weaknesses.[40] In Afghanistan and Iraq in the 2000s, the U.S. armed forces, though markedly improving, demonstrated and publicly acknowledged a lack of expertise in the early conduct of warfare against irregular enemies.[41] Irregular conflict, as in Iraq today, the U.S. Army's preferred type of war. This Army, at least until recently, has not been properly indoctrinated, equipped, and trained to succeed in Iraq. As much to the point, one must add, the soldiers have served generally faulty military strategy, and poor national security strategy, in ultimate pursuit of impractical policy goals. Strategy, operations, and tactics in Iraq all improved in 2007, culminated by claims of imminent military victory in late 2008, but it may well be the case that Iraqi internal political divisions will yet scuttle U.S. efforts.

Every layer in the national security architecture has to function effectively enough. Not perfectly; one must not seek an impossibly immaculate performance. No matter which desirable policy goals are chosen, and regardless of the theoretical wisdom in the selected strategy, to repeat, if the military machine cannot deliver sufficient success the entire project will fail. Culture, policy, strategy, operations, tactics, and logistics depend upon each other. The monumental task of combining policy intent with the necessary ways and means is the domain of strategy, both national security or grand, and military.

## Global Security and Future Warfare.

Clausewitz provides somber meditations on uncertainty, risk, chance, and friction as prominent features of warfare.[42] Of course, he is correct. But the great Prussian philosopher does bound his warnings, explicitly and implicitly. Notwithstanding his vigorous claim that "war is the realm of uncertainty" and his striking simile claiming that "[i]n the whole range of human activities, war most closely resembles a game of cards," his is not the counsel of despair in the face of a blind chance.[43] If we read *On War* carefully and reflect on the meaning of the whole book, it becomes obvious that the author judges governments and their military commanders to be far from helpless when chance strikes a potentially cruel blow.[44] First, Clausewitz praises a process of detailed war planning, hardly an activity that could be very valuable should chance reign supreme.[45] Second, he recognizes the role of genius in command as offering some protection against cruel strokes of fate.[46] Genius appears on a sliding scale of merit and requires a competent military instrument for its realization in action. Often it is said that operational planning is of more utility for the training of planners than for the plans that it yields.

Uncertainty is a feature of war, rendering warfare exceptionally difficult to treat analytically. Uncertainty can have a positive effect, as typically was claimed for nuclear deterrence.[47] But more generally it is a blight that cannot be treated conclusively. Because the future has not happened, defense planning cannot help becoming guesswork.[48] This guesswork generally is performed carefully, though one should never forget that the country's military posture ultimately is not the product strictly of a rational process of strategic net assessment. In addition, perhaps preponderantly, the posture is the result of an essentially political process keyed to questions of money. Of recent years, the U.S. defense community has taken the principle of uncertainty very much to heart. In fact, there is some danger that a prudent recognition of uncertainty may be accorded undue authority. As some scholars have begun to notice, although war is beset by nonlinearity, uncertainty, chance, and even chaotic conditions, by no means is it impervious to purposeful direction.[49] If it were, there could be no place for strategy. In historical practice, uncertainty, chance, and risk assuredly attend war and warfare, but they are simply conditions under which strategically educated leaders must labor. Clausewitz should not be characterized as a chaos theorist; he was not one such. To indicate how uncertain is the future, especially war in the future, is not to claim that the course of events is beyond shaping and even control.[50]

Empirical historical studies of defense planning, usually called war planning, are fairly rare. Single country works and treatises that are almost cookbooks on how to do it correctly, are far more common. It so happens that an edited book of unusual relevance to our concerns here has appeared recently. The previous major study a generation ago focused only on World War I: *War Plans of the Great Powers, 1880-1914*, edited by Paul M. Kennedy.[51] In contrast, the recent volume, *The Fog of Peace and War Planning: Military and Strategic Planning Under Uncertainty*, edited by Talbot C. Imlay and Marcia Duffy Toft, covers the great powers from

1815 to 1961.[52] Although the conclusions offered by the editors are less than startling, their brief introductory rumination is useful. For example, they offer the following nugget which combines the blindingly obvious with shrewd judgment:

> But if the task of military planning is indispensable, it is also fraught with an uncertainty rooted in three basic problems: that of identifying friend and foe, that of understanding the nature of future war, and that of determining its timing.
>
> Timing probably involves the greatest uncertainty. Aside from cases of deliberate aggression planners cannot confidently know whether war will break out tomorrow, next week, next year, or in the next decade.[53]

The implication of Imlay and Toft's statement is that war planning in peacetime cannot be performed efficiently.[54] The problem of deciding upon adequate defense preparation is the familiar one of insurance. How much protection should be purchased as a prudent hedge against threats that may never materialize?

In this monograph, unless otherwise specified, defense planning refers to what used to be, and in some quarters still is, known as war planning. This is planning for the country's overall defense posture, as well as military planning for operations at the high end of the operational spectrum. The text recognizes that the United States conducts planning at every level: from the political-policy, through the grand-strategic, to the military strategic, the theater—and lower, to the operational and tactical. In point of fact, the staffs in the vast multilayered bureaucracy of the U.S. Government, especially in its military institutions, write and rewrite plans of different kinds all the time.

Given that the mission here is to identify a sustainable national security strategy, the discussion of plans and planning generally refers to processes of discussion, decision, and action at that level.

It is well to develop and retain empathy for defense planners, because theirs is a necessary though awesomely challenging task. Because one is unavoidably ignorant about the future, that does not mean that the vital subjects of this section—global security and future warfare—can be neglected. Since one can only guess about the future of warfare, guess one must.[55] To cut to the chase, when one seeks a sustainable national security strategy, a hugely immodest project, what guidance can one seek, and from which sources? Must the future resemble the past? Unfortunately, history is all that is available for guidance. Yet "history" is not an objective record of who did what to whom, when, and why. Rather it is a confusion of competing historians who have told what they believed occurred. "The lessons of history" are notoriously short of authority.

Nonetheless, since the defense planners of today have to beware lest they project the current context mindlessly into the future, and can know nothing definite about the future, rival interpretations of the past are the only source of inspiration extant. Of course, one could sever the anchor chain to history and elect to go boldly into almost a wholly unfamiliar security future. It is possible, some would say desirable, to plan for a 21st century which bears little resemblance to the 20th and 19th. Attractive visions of global security radically different from current conditions are not hard to invent, but the appeal does not survive close study, at least it has yet to do so.[56]

American defense planners are required to think and prepare for a global domain. Even should a future U.S.

administration express an inward-looking domestic mood and attempt a significant reversal of today's forward presence, it would soon discover that its security concerns were distressingly global. The United States is too important an actor in all dimensions of world affairs, not least the financial and economic (e.g., maritime trade), to be able to pull up the drawbridge and mind its own business, inoffensively, in North America. This is not to claim that Americans have no choice in their national security policy, and hence strategy. But it does mean that because the country is the most essential of players in a global system of international relations, it must protect its vital national interests by accepting at least some measure of foreign engagement. How much, of what kind, and to what ends, are the issues here. Also, it is necessary never to forget the literally vital logistical dimension of national security strategy. Forward military deployment and basing are key enablers of strategic effectiveness.[57]

It is with some discomfort that I mix description with prediction and prescription. Indeed, I am generally altogether averse to prediction. However, at this juncture it is necessary to specify the working assumptions that should provide the bedrock, the firm footings, for the architecture of a sustainable American national security strategy. Although these are chosen strictly personally, they are widely shared, even if some readers find a few of them controversial. What should U.S. policymakers and military leaders assume about the future of global security and warfare? What do they believe they know about the future? Even if they are not at all certain, what do they choose to assume as a matter of prudence concerning distant hypothetical, threats. Here are six fundamental assumptions:

1. *War is endemic in the human condition.* Officials should not be distracted, let alone convinced, by

scholars who write about the transformation of war, about "new wars," about the end of war, or the end of major war as we have known it.[58] War, and its signature activity, warfare, quintessentially involving fighting and killing, are here to stay. Aside from the years of world war, the period since the end of the Cold War has been as bloody as any, and bloodier than most, in the 20th century. Those theorists, officials, and soldiers, who believed after 1991 that the future of conflict would be so constrained that Western forces would be limited to performing peacekeeping duties, Operations Other Than War (OOTW), and occasional brief fly-by bombardments, were seriously in error. Given the contemporary enthusiasm for military modernization around the world, except for EU-Europe, there is no doubt that this first assumption is near universally shared.

2. *Warfare will both evolve and appear in several forms.* Because of its superior investment in military technology, the United States is right to assume that it will lead the process of military innovation.[59] However, it is also correct in the relatively new assumption that advanced technology, though generally apt to be useful, cannot guarantee even tactical success, let alone operational, strategic or political.[60] Defense planners have to consider evolution in the "grammar" of war, as Clausewitz calls the mechanics of warfare, holistically.[61] The U.S. military establishment must recall old practices that were effective, as well as innovate, if it is to shine in future conflicts. The future is near certain to call on Americans to wage both regular and irregular warfare, often in the same trial of arms. In some cases, the United States will be able to choose the wars it fights in the 21st century; they will be wars of discretion. However, it would be an over-bold

prediction to claim that all of America's wars will be of that sort. Similarly, it would be rash indeed to predict that the character of America's future warfare will be dictated in the large by Americans. Adaptability has always been essential; it will remain so.

To record a worrying thought, Americans are so habituated to the blessings of technological superiority that they do not often consider the perils of nonlinear technical developments abroad that could place them behind the curve of innovation and its military exploitation. What if the next revolution in military affairs (RMA) leverages radically new technologies, and the leveraging is achieved preeminently by Chinese, Indians, or Europeans?[62] One brave but thoughtful prophet, Dale Walton, envisages with confidence the emergence of a new "technological 'super-revolution'." According to Walton, this "super-revolution," comprising "interrelated revolutions in biotechnology, nanotechnology, robotics, computer science, and other areas will result in extraordinarily potent war-fighting innovations."[63] Walton goes so far as to predict that "given the pace of technological change, it should be expected that within two decades a new RMA, the successor to the increasingly mature Second American RMA [nuclear and information technology], will be in evidence."[64]

One needs to consider as well the fact that we are still only at the beginning of the military space age, while cyber warfare, though already rife, is thoroughly immature. America may out-resource its actual and potential enemies by a country mile, but is it possible that those foes might invest more cunningly and effectively, especially in the uses to which new technology can be put? So many and unfamiliar are the military-technological possibilities of this century, that major outbreaks of warfare may be asymmetrical and historically nonlinear to the point of offering war-winning advantages to the more imaginative and innovative belligerent. This is not a prediction, but anyone obliged to think about future warfare would be foolish were he simply to assume that the United States will be wise and lucky in its technical, and consequential doctrinal, operational, and tactical choices.

3. *Global order is a meaningful concept: such order has to be policed by someone or something.* Global order is a value-charged idea, as is the claim that it needs to be kept. In practice, there may be extant no global condition that one could term orderly and no state, coalition, or international institution seeking to maintain order. By order, we understand a stable global context wherein the principal actors behave predictably in a manner that does not challenge the legitimacy or regular functioning of the prevailing pattern of international relations.[65] The United States has decided that terrorism, most especially Islamic fundamentalist terrorism, now commonly referred to as violent Islamism, is a threat to global order. More to the point, perhaps, since 1991, albeit not without a wobble or two, the United States has sought to play the thankless but self-flattering role of global guardian. Literally in every place in the world today that is experiencing serious instability, the United States is a relevant presence serving the American notion of order, arguably with the lonely exception of sub-Saharan Africa. While the United States is nominally committed to the concept of global order for its own sake, it has been most actively committed, as noted already, to advancing a desirable order through the promotion of democracy and open markets.

American national culture and world events have produced a situation wherein the United States is "globocop." Americans are combating the illegal drug industry in South and Central America (as well as in Afghanistan); through the North Atlantic Treaty Organization (NATO), they are on the line should the Russian Federation overreach in its harassment of the revived Baltic states, and one day possibly, Ukraine and Georgia; it is in the forefront of efforts to suppress violent Islamism in the Middle East, South Asia, and East Asia; and it is literally on the firing line in South Korea as well as prospectively in the Taiwan Straits. All of these and other dangerous tasks can be rationalized, and indeed may be judged sound, strategically, but, like the British Empire, they have been acquired piecemeal. Although the judgment bears hard on Americans, despite the pleasure of a sense of primacy, the global political system needs the United States as a policing agent. The system needs to be disciplined by some factor additional to the universal operation of enlightened self-interest and of good behavior norms as well as some "laws."

States or other communities need to be disciplined when they misbehave according to the standards that typically prevail, and indeed that need to prevail if the existing international order is to remain tolerably stable. In cases of minor transgressions, or of aggressive behavior by minor players, either international institutions or relatively strong regional powers may suffice to restore the status quo ante or compel a satisfactory compromise. But when the menace is on a scale, or has a geographical reach, that is more than local or minor, the United States at present is the only candidate for the role of global policeman on behalf, naturally, of its own notion of order.

The role is expensive and often unrewarding at best, and is certain periodically to be unpopular domestically. However, if the United States should decline to establish a forward presence around the world, off-shore or on-shore Eurasia, either materially or credibly in potential, then it would cease to be a shaping, let alone the most significant, factor in the future of international relations.

After Iraq, Americans could well decide that the possibilities of policy and strategic error are so large that the country should not trust itself to play the global guardian role. But one can predict that such a public policy mood would not long endure. The consequences of America-light purposeful behavior globally would come to be too uncomfortable for most Americans. Admittedly, this is a bold, perhaps rash, prediction. But it expresses the view that were the United States to disengage seriously from actual and potential security duties around Eurasia, it would soon regret the decision. This is not to neglect the possibility that elements of such a process of American disengagement from Eurasia, on-shore if not off-shore, might be compelled by the political decisions and strategic advances of others. Policy and strategy decisions may not be wholly discretionary for Washington.

4. *War entails warfare, and warfare always is about fighting.* Warfare is not only about fighting, but combat is the signature behavior of armies. Moreover, as Clausewitz, the master thinker, insists in much-quoted words: "The decision by arms is for all major and minor operations in war what cash payment is in commerce."[66] The U.S. armed forces currently are in no danger of neglecting their mandatory generic core competency — fighting. Leaders of all armed forces, everywhere, at least pay lip service to the connection between their profession and warfare, but many of them have no serious expectation of ever having to fire

30

shots in anger. Moreover, of those military institutions that do have grounds to anticipate action, the force in question is far more likely to be applied on behalf of domestic order than in the conduct of interstate war. Although American soldiers today are no strangers to warfare, it is a long time since they faced a first-class regular enemy, even a distinctly asymmetrical one.[67] It should be noted that all warfare is in some measure asymmetrical. The word is easily abused by overemployment. Not since 1953 in Korea have enemy aircraft occasionally been a nuisance to U.S. ground forces, while a context wherein the enemy held air superiority has not been suffered since 1943 in Sicily. America's foes in the GWOT or among the ranks of roguish states are sometimes cunning, reasonably well-trained, experienced, and exceedingly determined, all of which count for a lot. But they lack the resources to wage warfare on a major scale. Acquisition of WMD should greatly reduce the political and strategic disadvantages of such belligerents in the future, but this is still largely a future prospect. Of course, North Korea already has its nuclear equalizer, and Iran is well on the way to acquiring one also.

It has been a long time since the warriors of the United States have had to fight an enemy of approximately the same military weight, even if that enemy were to fight in a style that was highly asymmetrical. In World War II by 1943-45, the Wehrmacht needed to seek compensation for U.S., British, and Russian material superiority in its tactical skill, sheer determination, well-chosen terrain to defend, and some equipment quality edge. Of necessity, it waged a poor man's style of regular warfare. American soldiers, making the prudent assumption that there will be "regular" fighting in their future, should not assume that materially well-endowed regular foes will fight in ways symmetrical to U.S. preferences and expectations.[68]

Assumptions are cultural, or nearly such, and do not alter readily, even in the face of evidence suggesting they are ill-founded.[69] As many commentators have noticed, it has long been assumed by the U.S. armed forces that real warfare was regular in character. Today there is some danger that that assumption has been dropped in favor of an expectation of COIN and CT. As a corrective to the previous assumption, some swing in the direction of the irregular end of the combat spectrum is welcome. However, it is unsafe to assume that America's strategic history will be principally concerned with warfare against enemies who must fight irregularly. On the one hand, there is a full house of potentially hostile states emerging in world politics. On the other hand, it is neither desirable nor politically feasible for the U.S. armed forces to be committed principally to the conduct of major COIN and CT campaigns.

By all means American soldiers should seek to improve their understanding of the cultural dimension of warfare. But one cannot expect and should not seek a transformation in the American way of war in favor of general prowess in irregular warfare. The U.S. armed forces are sufficiently large to be able to afford specialized capability for COIN and CT. Military force, U.S. style, is strong on maneuver, certainly on movement, and firepower. This style is not tailor-made for the conduct of counterirregular warfare, although it has its place, as does technological sophistication despite its limitations. Most of the U.S. armed forces are designed to meet and defeat other regular forces. They should remain tilted thus in their competencies. Certainly they can acquire and hone skills at COIN and

CT, and they should increase their cultural awareness, as indeed is occurring today. First and foremost, though, they need to remain an adaptable instrument for combat against states.

5. *New first-class competitors/enemies will emerge (indeed, are emerging already).* Some Americans have been so smitten with the ideology of primacy, despite the experience in Iraq since 2003, that they cannot quite sign on to the assumption that a worthy "super" enemy or coalition of enemies will emerge over the next several decades. But such an emergence is precisely the prediction on the part of the author, and it is a current assumption of many, though by no means all, of America's strategic theorists and commentators. Understandably and probably wisely, the government is publicly uncommitted on the subject of the duration of the American hegemony. Obviously, American officials do not wish to predict their country's decline and fall from ascendancy.

Regional great powers such as China, India, Russia, possibly EU-Europe, Brazil, and Iran, among others, must balance the value of a faraway U.S. hegemon with a distant homeland, against the political insult and damage to local ambitions and interests that such a hegemon inflicts. Americans can assume with confidence that their current global role as guardian of order increasingly will be opposed by rising states and coalitions, most especially in East Asia. However, it is necessary to remember that this region, the emerging center of world politics and the most dynamic source of economic globalization, has its own rivalries and may be able to provide a regional balance of power even without active U.S. participation. Because of a long-time focus on Europe and the Middle East, many American analysts are wont to forget the unique geography, geopolitics, and geostrategic conditions of East and South Asia. The distances are immense, with the regions and subregions divided by extensive forbidding terrain—desert, mountains, jungle—and with the commercial and military contexts being largely geographically maritime. East Asia is about as different from Europe as it can be, geographically and politically.[70] Moreover, as Dale Walton perceptively observes, East Asia is not a potential power vacuum, even should the United States greatly reduce its forward presence.[71] China, India, and Japan (not to mention Russia and Indonesia) are likely to prove more than capable of balancing each other. Indeed, if one is worried about a credibly potential 1914 scenario in the 21st century, indigenous East Asian balance of power politics is probably the subject to examine.[72]

6. *Surprise happens*. Finally, since uncertainty now is accorded its official due if not more than it merits, it is reasonable to claim that U.S. defense planners recognize the certainty of future major surprises, favorable and otherwise.[73] The future of warfare will record extensive activity all along the spectrum of regularity-irregularity; no surprise there. But, it is also very likely to contain some RMAs. Given the contemporary immaturity of biotechnology, space technology, and cyber technology, it is not exactly a bold leap into the unknown to predict further technology-led RMAs. Actually, it is unconvincing to predict that warfare of most kinds will not be reshaped by biotechnology, nanotechnology, robotics, and information technology (IT), just to cite the more obvious technical baskets.[74] Given that the U.S. defense community, along with the Chinese, Russian, Indian, and many others, currently is still low on the learning curve for the confident conduct of cyber warfare, just one area of certain technical

progress, the perils of specific prediction become all too obvious. The United States has to assume that technology, culture (including political beliefs), and diplomatic ties, as well as the consequences of climate change, hold some nonlinearities that will threaten to make the expectations of so-called long-term planners appear distinctly foolish. So it was in the 19th and 20th centuries. There is thus every reason to believe that the 21st will significantly discomfort U.S. defense planners.[75]

## The American Role.

What should be the American role in a future world that could well be as dangerous, if not more so, than that described and analyzed above? To behave in such a manner that the U.S. national interest, singular and plural, is best protected and advanced, of course. But how should that be done?—that is the question. Perhaps the first epigraph of this monograph provides the vital clue: "If American hegemony is the answer, what is the question?" The Bush administration of 2002-03 vintage was in no doubt that active U.S. leadership in the world was essential. Such forthright behavior, expressing a global moral and material primacy— hegemony was not a favored term—was required in order to ensure America's safety. The vicious assaults of 9/11 and the previous outrages in New York City and in Africa in the 1990s were undoubtedly a challenge to the United States. But did they amount to a dare to the country to wage a GWOT? Was it not more likely that a global American response which favored military intervention, forcible regime change, and other actions of a violent character, was almost exactly the reaction that fanatical Islamists sought to trigger? After all, their real target is the House of Islam, not the purportedly decadent societies of West (and East). Be that as it may, the United States chose to pick up the gauntlet and join global battle with al-Qaeda, its associates, and its imitators.

As the more perceptive of American commentators have noted, U.S. national security policy in the 2000s, though not necessarily its strategy, is heavily influenced by the national culture. Some of the persisting features of American culture produce the appearance and reality of history repeating itself. As this monograph seeks to divine the future of U.S. national security strategy and seeks in particular to discover the necessary elements for sustainability, the cultural contribution looms ever larger.

Compare the following statements, one by a president who has become iconic and in life was a conservative Democrat, the other by a president who at present is less than iconic in a positive sense and is a muscular liberal Republican (on foreign policy). In his Inaugural Address on January 21, 1961, John F. Kennedy made the following solemn pledge: "We shall pay any price, bear any burden, meet any hardship, support any friend, oppose any foe to assure the survival and the success of liberty."[76] This was not hollow rhetoric. It reflected American values and self-confidence. Vietnam was not the inevitable consequence of the pledge, and others in similar vein, but the many decisions that led to America's decade-long war in South East Asia were enabled by the global role thus identified. To fast-forward to June 1, 2002, one finds President George W. Bush declaring thus: "We will defend the peace by fighting terrorists and tyrants. We will preserve the peace by building good relations among the great powers. We will extend the peace by encouraging free and open societies on every continent."[77]

In that same seminal document, *The National Security Strategy of the United States of America* (September 2002), President Bush could hardly have been clearer in his mixture of hard-headed realism and crusading liberalism. "The U.S. national security strategy will be based on a distinctly American internationalism that reflects the union of our values and our national interests. *The aim of this strategy is to help make the world not just safer but better.*"[78]

And how is this to be accomplished? The answer is by the global promotion of the Big Three Values— "freedom, democracy, and free enterprise." Based on the Big Three just quoted, President Bush declared, "The great struggles of the 20th century between liberty and totalitarianism ended with a decisive victory for the forces of freedom—and a single sustainable model for national success," As we observed about the often-quoted Kennedy pledge, these and many parallel declarations by George W. Bush were sincere expressions of the core liberal values of American national culture. In addition, as with the Kennedy Inaugural, they signaled a serious policy mood and, at least by implication, the character of future national security strategy.

Before confronting the apparent and the real range of American choice over its future national security policy, it is necessary to make three general observations on the nature and character of policy. First, there is the fundamental matter of definition. This monograph insists that policy is restricted to the purposes to which national agents, civilian and military, are committed with variable enthusiasm. To risk muddying the water a little, as a preliminary matter it is appropriate to recognize the common sense in the trinitarian explanation that policy is "capabilities, declarations, and actions."[80] In other words, policy is what one can do. No matter how elevated the authority of their utterer, words cannot convey policy if, logically and plausibly, they are contradicted by the evidence of capabilities and behavior. The trinity "capabilities, declarations, and actions" was not offered by its author, Morton Halperin, as a scholarly definition of policy, but rather as a potent dose of realism. Policy should not be defined strictly by instrumental behavior, but neither can its merit and authority be unaffected by strategic choice and operational and tactical prowess.[81]

Second, while policy can turn on a dime, as the old saying goes, the major capabilities available to strategy to advance policy will have lead-times that typically are measured in several years. One frequent consequence of this temporal fact of life is that by the time the capabilities' answer is reasonably mature, the strategy and policy question will have changed almost beyond recognition. By way of illustration, in the 1990s and 2000s, U.S., other NATO, Russian, and Eastern European (ex-Warsaw Pact) armed forces were heavily equipped to perform vanished missions. In addition, many of those countries were inextricably committed to the pursuit of military programs less than optimal for the post-Cold War security environment. The fall of the Soviet Union was a de facto geopolitical and geostrategic revolution. But military establishments, especially in NATO, could not transform themselves on anything close to the same time scale. Moreover, given the rapidity with which the political context can alter, it is probably just as well that material military conditions most typically shift gradually and only incrementally. Given the cost and complexity of today's major high-technology military programs, a true military transformational project could require several decades to complete. In historical practice, technical innovation and military postural change are usually more cumulative than nonlinear.

Third, the range of practical choice in strategy, and hence policy, at any point in time must be constrained by physical/material — including human — realities. That fact is commonly appreciated. Less well recognized, however, is the easily attestable fact that policy choice usually is similarly restricted to only a modest pace of change. It is rare for the policy reviews so beloved by each new administration to produce anything bold and original, no matter how dazzling the labels and extravagant the claims. There are excellent reasons why this should be so. Preeminently Americans, but others as well, are moved to decide and behave by broad motives that are readily summarized in the Thucydidean triptych of "fear, honor, and interest."[82] Generally speaking, there will be many more, and more important, continuities than discontinuities from administration to administration. Permeating and in good part shaping U.S. choice of national security policy will be the three most relevant categories of American culture: public/national, strategic, and military.[83] Scholars will identify extensive U.S. discretion in the selection of its role in the world. Most of this declared range of policy discretion, however, is strictly illusory.

To be sustainable, a chosen role in the world and the national security strategy that supports it have to be both culturally acceptable at home as well as successful abroad. Americans are not at liberty to play which global role they prefer, in whatever manner they choose. The outside world is always likely to resist, to push back. Officially, one must identify the national role before the national strategy, a batting order followed here and in the closing section. However, the role cannot be selected prudently without reference to feasible strategy. And feasible strategy depends in substantial part upon the practicality of the necessary ways, methods, and mobilization of the essential means. These means will be both material and "moral" or cultural (e.g., domestic political support, reflecting a resonance with national values).

Despite the fashionable and sometimes superficially plausible view that America can choose its preferred role in the world, we must reiterate that the country's freedom of global action in practice is severely constrained by factors beyond its control. The sources of this constraint are both domestic and foreign. Other scholars will design their own short list of alternatives for the U.S. role in the world of the 21st century. But however the cake is cut, the total content generally is the same. The discussion here finds it useful to identify four master conceptual options for the U.S. role.

1. *Hegemony—primacy for global guardianship.* This has been the explicit U.S. choice since 2002. Once the dust was well settled from the collapse of the twin towers in New York, the Bush administration decided that America's security could be assured only according to a standard for order operative in a truly global context. Moreover, this order could be policed and advanced only if the United States is prepared to be globally proactive. Washington recognized that the United States is the sole candidate for global leadership, the hegemonic role. Also, it concluded that this role allows, indeed obliges, America to take the cultural offensive. The world has to be made safe for democracy, liberty, free enterprise, and free trade. Not only must the nonstate or rogue state enemies of

these values be confronted and eliminated, but the greater states must cooperate with a U.S.-led mission to improve the world.

2. *Anti-hegemonial off-shore balancer and spoiler.* After Iraq, the United States may tire of the on-shore hegemonic role in Eurasia, without necessarily wishing to withdraw from fairly active participation in global security affairs. As a consequence, as Barry Posen argues, it should concentrate on exploitation of its military-technological strengths by domination of the global geographical and geostrategic "commons" consisting of the sea, air, space, and cyberspace.[84] Events on and in contested and contestable continental terrain in Eurasia-Africa in particular, Sir Halford Mackinder's "World-Island," would be influenced both by power exercised from a distance (e.g., naval firepower and long-range air and missile strikes) and through local and regional allies. The United States would strive to remain the most potent state in the world, but it would not intend to intervene to achieve continental regime change. Indeed, the country would be most careful to avoid foreign missions that could lead to ground commitments, especially ones that plausibly could become protracted. The U.S. role would be to serve as an extremely heavyweight potential ally should a region be menaced by the ambition of a would-be regional or global hegemon. The United States would not seek to play global hegemon, but in its own interest it would intend to spoil the prospect of hegemonic success for any other great state or coalition. The U.S. role in the world of anti-hegemonial off-shore balancer and spoiler is essentially negative. It would aim to protect America by preventing the emergence and maturation of a potentially globally dominant strategic competitor. U.S. continental behavior beyond

the Americas would be limited to modest assistance and advice.[85]

3. *Disengaged lone wolf for only minimal participation in international military security affairs.* American culture has always favored a noticeable measure of national isolation from the polluting entanglements of the extra-American world. The United States is not only culturally an affirmation of faith in a better, even divinely inspired, society. It is also a cultural rejection of the "Old World." Americans know they cannot be rigorously isolated in North America in this globalized era. But they are certainly willing to be persuaded that they have the practical option of massively reducing their overseas security commitments. With the greatest army, navy, air force, and, eventually, space forces in the world, and with an economy and currency upon which world trade, and hence development and prosperity, depend, the United States has a "lone wolf" option. So, at least, it can be argued.

4. *Moderate competitor and partner in a multipolar world.* This fourth option is becoming increasingly popular, even fashionable. It has flourished in reaction to what is regarded widely as the relatively ineffective and counterproductive unilateralism of recent U.S. foreign policy and strategy (national and military). Also, plausible anticipations of the rise of East and South Asia relative to North America and Europe have led many scholars and commentators to believe that 21st century America is going to have to learn to coexist with near peers in a multipolar world. Whether Americans like it or not, the argument goes, the United States will be obliged to share with others the most senior security assignment as guardian of global order. This will not be another "American century." The only room for doubt today is whether the United States

will find itself locked into yet another prolonged and bilateral superpower struggle, this time with China, or whether the global competition will be multipolar. It is almost certainly true that at the present time, influenced overwhelming by the Afghan and Iraqi experiences, a large majority of American foreign policy and strategic commentators believe that the United States: (1) is well advanced in the process of losing its briefly hegemonic status; (2) is condemned to pursue a national security policy and strategy that gives pride of place to multilateral cooperation rather than unilateral action; and (3) has no choice other to accept as an unwelcome fact the imminent arrival of a genuinely multipolar (or at least bipolar) world. There may be more American scholarly and popular adherents to the vision of a multipolar than a bipolar security future.

What is one to make of the options outlined above as candidates for America's role in the world? This monograph will risk being out of step with politically correct opinion by endorsing a variant of the first option, hegemony-primacy for global guardianship. Contrary to appearances, perhaps, this is a scholarly professional judgment, not a visceral patriotic one. In addition, I am convinced that the continued conduct of a policy of hegemony-primacy, provided it is adapted in the light of Iraq and Afghanistan, is the only practicable and sustainable U.S. policy option for the future. The prime objection to options one, two, and three is that none of them will work. Each is either culturally unsustainable at home in America, or is near certain to be ineffective abroad, or both. The role of "off-shore balancer-spoiler" ignores the lessons of historical experience. The United States will have foreign continental interests that are deemed vital, and those interests can be secured only by a serious presence on the ground. In the immortal words of a wise American sailor: *"The ultimate determinant in war is the man on the scene with a gun . . . this is the soldier."*[86] Fly-by presence and bombardment from afar cannot yield the quality of political control that Americans will find they need. As for the coalition "spoiler" dimension to this role, it might succeed, but then again it might not. An America that declines virtually all continental commitment, even NATO obligations, would not be likely to succeed as an effective makeweight to assist regional states in their attempts to frustrate others' hegemonic ambition.

The "lone wolf" America that elects to withdraw from active global security engagement would discover that its attempt to be disinterested in the extra-American world was damaging to the country's interests. Also, such an American policy could not long endure because it would be rejected culturally by many Americans. Although American culture favors limited liability abroad, it still demands to be spread so as to colonize a world that stubbornly remains backward. Almost regardless of material considerations, too many Americans want to improve the outside world for wholehearted security withdrawal to be sustainable.

As for the American policy envisaging the country as a balance-of-power player in a multipolar world, it is likely to be both unnecessary as well as culturally infeasible. "Rise of . . ." predictions are generally not implausible, at least with respect to China and India. But both seem likely to be regional super-states rather than global peers of the United States. When one looks for other "poles" for this hypothetical global security system, the tale becomes even less convincing than it is for China and India. For the leading cases,

Russia has motive, will, and much geography, but it has systemic weaknesses fatal to its ambitions. Japan has much of the making of a superpower, but it has an immense dependency on overseas suppliers, which is a potentially lethal vulnerability. Chinese naval, air, and missile power lies athwart the lines of commercial supply of most of Japan's oil and gas. EU-Europe could become a regional and even a global superpower on all dimensions, but this possibility currently is a light year from contemporary political and military realization. Elsewhere, one can cite Iran, perhaps Egypt and Brazil, but at most they could aspire only to be great in their own neighborhoods. None appear to bear the promise of being able to function as one among a handful of global or supra-regional "poles."

To conclude this analysis of the future American role in the world, we must specify the reasons for our choice of the option one variant "hegemony-primacy-light" as the preferable master concept for the U.S. role. The first epigraph of this monograph posed a fundamental question: "If American hegemony is the answer, what is the question?" The question is, "Who or what maintains order in world politics?" If "maintains" is too strong a term, acceptable alternatives would be "guards" or "supports." Two empirically founded assumptions drive this analysis. First, a reasonably orderly world is possible only if it is policed by a hegemonic power or alliance, a leader. Second, at present only the United States is capable of playing the global hegemonic role.

We specify "hegemony-primacy-light" because the U.S. role in the world requires each of the three qualities. To be the leader, the hegemon, the United States needs to sustain its primacy in several dimensions of power. Along with a technological long suit, civilian and military, and the  large size of its economy, a global leader must be militarily preeminent broadly speaking, as well as the wielder of potent cultural soft power. Of course, military preeminence may not be fully comprehensive, while cultural dynamism and attractiveness can disappointingly create hostile alien cultural "blowback." By specifying hegemony-primacy-*light*, we mean that American hegemony has to be a primacy expressed more in leadership than in actual application of the mailed fist. The latter will not succeed if it is the principal weapon in the U.S. strategy arsenal, nor if it is employed with little discrimination among cases. American military power is absolutely essential as the option of last resort, but it is more potent as threat than it is in action. Force should be regarded primarily as a vital aid to U.S. hegemonic statecraft, not as the lifeblood of hegemony. It should not be America's default option. "When in doubt, kill people and inflict damage," is not a wise precept.

History shows that a world-ordering role needs to be performed, like it or not. If no state, alliance, institutional complex, or set of norms and laws operates to regulate and discipline international behavior, the result is anarchy. To repeat, the job needs to be done. As hegemon by self-appointment from a field of only one, the United States strives to deny operating space and opportunity for roguish behavior by others. Many Americans have difficulty with this limited remit, but the U.S. hegemon can play only an enabling role on behalf of its values of liberty, democracy, and the practice of free market economics, it cannot impose them.

Other states will compete, indeed already are competing, with the United States. Hegemony is not a divine bequest which, duly delivered, means the end of history.[87] Currently the United States has a lengthy lead in the factors that contribute to national power, but it is being eroded by the focused efforts of others, and even by the long familiar historical cycle wherein polities rise and fall as if by natural causes. Reasons contributing to a relative American decline would include "imperial overstretch,"[88] the attempt to do too much with too little, and the jealousy of others, *their* "fear, honor, and interest." Through wise statecraft and some good fortune America may be able to stretch its hegemonic moment well into the 21st century. Alternatively, a combination of foreign policy defeats, relative economic and financial set-backs, and skillful anti-hegemonic behavior by rivals, may bring America's global leadership to an untimely end. This would be a great misfortune for the whole world, because the United States is a distinctly benign hegemon, as hegemons go. And it is far from obvious that a global security context bereft of American leadership could possibly be an improvement upon the conditions of today.

It is essential for the makers of U.S. national security policy never to forget that effective global policing, in common with all policing, must rest upon a broad communal consent. Rogues and would-be rogues, state and nonstate, can be kept in line and if necessary be forcibly reeducated only if the guardian of order enjoys the consent, the confidence, of the general community. U.S. policy for global order does not need a universal approval, but it must be manifest in goals and behavior that the generality of players, globally, accept as legitimate and desirable. In short, in its foreign policy the United States has to serve a general good as well as itself.

The hegemonic role in the 21st century has nothing to do with the acquisition of territorial empire. The only empire that interests the United States today is the support of an expanding community of like-value polities. The problems with the U.S. hegemonic role are the product of a combination of human error (e.g., cultural hubris) by American policymakers and the structure of world politics. These are not trivial sources of difficulty. For a leading example, one can argue that the United States did the right thing with its invasion of Iraq, but it did it for the wrong reasons and, in the crucial opening months after the military victory, mainly in the wrong way.[89] The principal source of difficulty for the U.S. hegemonic role is the fact that great states are rarely content to acquiesce in an international security system organized, led, and reflecting the values and interests of another power. To name names, China today is not interested in establishing a global imperium, but it is firmly committed to the dismantlement of American leadership and guardianship of global order, most especially in its own neighborhood in East Asia.[90] China may not be overly interesting in fighting to become Number One, but it is resolute in rejecting the humiliating status of being Number Two.

As was noted earlier, this monograph is underimpressed with the attractions, either for Americans or for the world at large, of an emergent multipolar global security system. A key assumption behind the multipolar theory has to be that the polar players would be approximately equal in strength and influence. Also, it is assumed that in addition to the global players balancing each other, they would function collectively if competitively in a manner loosely reminiscent of the Concert of Europe in the 19th century.[91] Leaving aside reasons to doubt the efficacy of the historical Concert, such a notion is deeply unsatisfactory for the future. To summarize the problems with a multipolar 21st century: it would be resisted by a majority of Americans, who are habituated both materially and culturally to primacy, or at least to preeminence; it would not work as the leading mechanism for global security; and a multipolar world would be prone to outbreaks of both regional and global warfare.

To focus on just one of the problems of multipolarity, the great power players would each be far more devoted to improving their own competitive position than guarding the values and structure of global security. When no single state is predominant, it can never be clear who should act to maintain and restore order. Everyone will try to play "free-rider." History and logic demonstrate the truth of this fatal deficiency. Consider the contemporary cases of North Korea and Iran. At present, it is unlikely that action will be taken to disarm either country of its actual or in-process and forthcoming nuclear weapons. But today, at least, it is plain beyond doubt exactly who needs to act, should military action be essential. In a multipolar system, rogues and other menaces behave as they wish for a long time, safe in the knowledge that they are the targets of empty threats and interminable diplomacy. A multipolar world is a world without a sheriff.

Regarded systemically, the principal function of a hegemonic power is to undertake those truly hard tasks that no one else can attempt with a good prospect of success, even were they willing. The posse will ride only if it is led by a sheriff. This monograph thus takes the position that a U.S. decision to acquiesce quietly in, even encourage, the emergence of a multipolar world (the United States, China, Russia, India, Japan, EU-Europe?) would be a serious mistake. A multipolar security system would not generate security, quite the reverse. It would not work in the fashion that history-minded theorists anticipate. Even worse, it would constitute and promote a context ripe for the return of great power wars.

Afghanistan and Iraq in the 2000s do not demonstrate the folly of American global hegemony, or even the lack of wisdom in a forward strategy for global security. Instead, these protracted episodes show yet again what all of history can tell us. Specifically, policy and strategy errors can be punished severely. Policymakers and generals make mistakes, in common with the rest of us. The test of their fitness for responsibility is their ability to learn from error and adapt.[92] America's mistakes in Afghanistan and Iraq have been of kinds endemic to major military interventions in foreign societies through the ages. Unfortunately, many of those among us who currently are hostile to the U.S. mission in Iraq, appeal to nonexistent alternatives for the U.S. role in the world. Even if one were certain that U.S. policy on Iraq has been marked by a series of mistakes, it would not justify a violent swing in national policy. There is no promising alternative global security system, just waiting to kick in once Washington abandons its recent unilateralist tendency. The section that follows argues that the United States requires the services of a sustainable national security strategy, rather than a radical and impractical shift in national security policy.

## The Components of a Sustainable National Security Strategy.

What is the strategy that could sustain the national security policy of "hegemony-light?" Put more usefully, what are the principal components and features of such a strategy? On the basis of the preceding analysis, the character of such a strategy has become clear. This section describes its make-up.

The U.S. hegemon needs to be able to control the geographies of the global commons.[93] Americans will have to be free to use the sea, the air, space, and cyberspace at will, all the while being able to deny such operational liberty to some other states and political entities. If this demanding multienvironmental requirement cannot be met, the United States could, and probably would, be unable to function strategically as the leading guardian of global order. This role demands the ability to exercise global access for power projection, even against sophisticated access denial capabilities and strategies. For example, attempts by U.S. airpower to secure and exploit control would certainly be contested in large areas of continental airspace. An emerging super-state as well as regional great powers could mount nontrivial opposition with well-networked air defense systems. Strategically, the relative significance of each geography varies from case to case.

However, given American geography and geopolitics, it is a permanent U.S. geostrategic requirement to command transit, globally by sea and air, as well as in orbit and through the "infosphere" electronically.[94] It has yet to be demonstrated, or even argued plausibly, that cyberspace is uniquely challenging in some vital regard. Should the control of cyberspace be impossible or only limited, the global sheriff could find itself unable to function effectively. It follows that the subject of cyberwar is in need of the most urgent attention, given current uncertainties and unknowns. Although control of the commons is essential strategically, it can be only instrumental. No one can inhabit these unfriendly environments. American strategy is indeed blessed with geographical, cultural, and technological advantages that facilitate control, but as British naval historian and theorist Sir Julian Corbett wrote a century ago:

> Since men live upon the land and not upon the sea, great issues between nations at war have always been decided—except in the rarest of cases—either by what your army can do against your enemy's territory and national life, or else by the fear of what the fleet makes it possible for your army to do.[95]

Technological progress brought airpower, space-power, and cyberpower, and also greatly enhanced the potency of the navy in power projection. Nonetheless, Corbett's claim retains most of its plausibility. The American hegemon must use the global commons in order to achieve distant influence. For that purpose, some local continental presence is necessary.

To be effective as the global leader or hegemon, the United States needs to be able to dissuade, deter, and, if necessary, defeat any rival state or coalition. This is a hugely demanding role which obliges adoption of a strategy, and the development and maintenance of armed forces, that literally must be second to none. If the United States could be challenged and either faced down diplomatically on a matter of vital global interest, or bested militarily, it would not remain hegemon for long. A regional or even a local power, let alone a territorially elusive nonstate entity, may prove impossible to dissuade or deter, as well as difficult to defeat in combat. Nonetheless, a hegemonic America must be able to win in regular warfare of all kinds and at least perform competently and creditably in irregular hostilities. An occasional defeat is bearable, provided the country learns from its mistakes. If the United States were incapable of deterring or defeating a rising super state, except perhaps with a great deal of assistance from allies, the global security order would have become bipolar or multipolar. A bipolar or multipolar international order could be stable in their different ways, but those ways would be judged undesirable by most Americans. In the medium and especially the long runs, the United States will have no choice other than to share its global influence more and more. However, for reasons already specified here, such a condition should not be hastened or welcomed.

American national security strategy and forces must be adaptable. This should be so obvious and basic a point as to warrant the charge of banality. Strategy and defense planning are very much about the making of choices that must impose opportunity costs as well as benefits. As was noted much earlier, when citing the conclusions to some excellent historical studies of peacetime war planning, key decisions on strategy, doctrine, and capabilities often have to be made in the face of profound ignorance over the identity of enemies, the character of future warfare, and—above all else—the timing of active hostilities.[96] Do U.S. forces need to be able to go literally anywhere, fight anybody, and win at acceptable cost? For the global sheriff, the answer has to be "yes," even though one recognizes that such a demand for universally successful performance is unrealistic.

Regular conventional warfare currently is America's military long suit. Some, perhaps many, military experts believe that such warfare belongs only in the past. Technology, culture, and politics have effectively retired battle between uniformed armed forces according to this view. The master narrative for the 21st century is, and will be, "war amongst the people."[97] At least, this is the fashionable theory. Obviously, if regular, largely meaning interstate, wars do not lurk to ambush us in the future, we should not expend scarce resources preparing for them. But how certain can one be that interstate war is obsolete?[98] Is it not likely that the theory of an exclusively irregular future for warfare reflects nothing much more solid than a simplistic extrapolation of recent and current history into an inherently unknowable future? This author is not persuaded that America's strategic future will be strictly confined to conflict with enemies who must fight in irregular modes. Since the world continues to be organized and dominated by at least semi-sovereign states and given that there will be ample issues to fuel rivalries, it is only prudent to continue to emphasize the necessity for excellence in regular, if sometimes asymmetrical, styles of combat.

COIN and CT are important, indeed vital, core competencies for the U.S. armed forces and other security agencies. They need to be accepted as permanent missions. This does not mean, however, that irregular warfare will, or should, dominate America's medium- and long-term strategic future. COIN ought to be a competency which specialized elements of the armed forces perform well. It is necessary for most of those armed forces to concentrate on regular, if asymmetrically-conducted, combat in all geographical environments. Also, it is important that the United States not make a habit of undertaking the thankless task of attempting, in notable part forcibly, to remake alien societies into "better" places. Because of its liberal culture, married to apparent opportunity, the United States cannot eschew being a force for "good" in the world. But this culturally propelled mission generally should not be promoted by military activity, at least not directly. American national security strategy should be geared to preparation for interstate conflict, not to enforcing benign regime change in societies that Americans scarcely comprehend. The largely interdependent cultural values of liberty, democracy, and the free market must be promoted by Americans, if only because these values are expressions of American self-identity. To say that, though, is not to endorse, let alone require, a national security strategy of liberation and moral improvement abroad. Such a strategy must fail, because it demands of the agencies for U.S. policy a cultural effect they cannot deliver, save rarely. The prudent statesman plays according to the odds that derive from experience and logic. Success in the remaking of foreign societies is a mission that inherently commands only very long odds.

Exploiting their superiority on and in the varied geographies that comprise the global commons, the U.S. armed forces need to acquire and perfect what one can term a decisive raiding capability. Americans should strive hard to avoid commitment to protracted and complex operations on land. But they will derive great strategic, and hence political, advantage from the ability to intervene in foreign lands swiftly and decisively on a strike-and-depart basis. It should go without saying that the adoption of a raiding strategy as an important component and expression of national security strategy has to be nested in a holistic approach to conflict. This is not to suggest that American soldiers should be employed simply to create brief mayhem and then leave the mess for others to clean up. The argument, rather, is that in its policing role as hegemon-light, the United States should seek to avoid lengthy land campaigning. Contemporary experience with Iraq, whatever the outcome may prove to be, is an exemplar of behavior that the United States should strive hard to avoid.

For many years to come, on any plausible assay, America will remain globally ascendant. But the country would soon find itself suffering from a severe case of the malady of "imperial overstretch" that historian Paul Kennedy popularized in the late 1980s, were it to make a habit of its Iraqi and Afghan experiences.[99] A wise statesman plays to his country's strengths, not its relative limitations. The rapid projection of military power is, or should be, a key American strength. But to exploit this unique American capability safely, there is a need for political, indeed even cultural, discipline. Almost inevitably, military intervention to solve a pressing security problem invites mission leap, let alone mission creep, when political temptation is provided by initial military success.

Because America's hegemonic strength invites rivals and outright enemies to compete and fight asymmetrically, Americans need to sustain not only technological leadership, but also, of even greater significance, intellectual leadership in strategic theory and doctrine. Both ideas and technology matter, but of the two, ideas matter most. If the United States should suffer severe military setbacks in the future, most likely the reason will not be some technological shortfall, but rather that familiar machines and forces are employed in unexpected ways by the enemy. Such ways could reflect military cultural differences between societies, or they might just be the product of clever strategy designed to outflank predictable American military behavior.

To be sustainable, national security strategy must be truly "national" or "grand." It is an all too prevalent error for policymakers to depend narrowly upon the military dimension to such strategy. Military power is most potent when its employment remains only potential as a brooding possibility. It is a familiar mistake in statecraft for policymakers to reach for their gun too rapidly in quest of swift success. Diplomacy and nonviolent coercion, as well as bribery, can appear distinctly inferior instruments when compared with the promise of cutting the Gordian Knot with a quick and decisive military victory. As we have noted, national security strategy is a slippery subject. Frequently it is confused with foreign policy, with military strategy, or with military operations. National security strategy must have a domestic as well as an external dimension. It has to be acceptable to the values of national public culture, national strategic culture, and military-institutional cultures. At the same time, of course, the strategy needs to address the country's foreign strategic problems effectively. This point amounts to a reminder that national security strategy has many components in addition to the military. There has to be a plausible possibility of armed conflict for an issue to be addressed by national security strategy, but the military component need not predominate.

A sustainable strategy will reflect policy goals and tactical military behavior that do not give gross offense either to domestic cultural, or to international, norms of tolerable conduct. The more consent America attracts abroad, the greater the practical assistance upon which the country will be able to draw and the more likely that U.S. policy will succeed.[100] If this sometimes elusive condition is met, American strategy should prove sustainable.

A vital component of national security strategy is the dialogue that strategists must maintain both with policy and with operations and tactics. Strategy is the bridge between means and ends. If these dialogues are absent, intermittent, or severely flawed, the prospects

57

for national success will not be high. It is only the strategy function that binds together the country's means and ends. Strategists devise the methods, the "ways," that enable the coercive agencies, including preeminently the military establishment, to pursue objectives that should translate ultimately into desired political effects. The practical difficulties that commonly inhibit or frustrate the dialogue component of strategy are typically underestimated or simply ignored.[101] Only exceptionally are policymakers today well-educated in military matters, while the military profession can be disinclined to say "no" to the civil power. In America, soldiers obey orders from civilians, they do not make policy. This is an oversimplification, but it remains the ideal of American civil-military relations.[102] In practice, the strategist must aim to educate the civilian policymaker as to what the military instrument can and cannot do. This is vital. Because history is not strictly linear and predetermined, it will often be far from obvious just what soldiers might be able to deliver by way of strategic and political effects. The theory of strategy says far too little about the subject's difficulties. Even the discussion in Clausewitz's *On War* is inadequate.[103] For national security strategy to be successful and sustainable, it has to be nurtured on a metaphorical bridge. On this bridge, the civilian policymaker and the professional soldier meet, exchange information, and, through the alchemy required of the strategist and strategy, produce coherent and well directed intentions, sometimes leading to military action.

## Conclusions and Recommendations.

1. *"Hegemony-light" is a policy, not a strategy.* The main reason why the United States should endeavor to remain the hegemon is the need to play the dominant role in the endless struggle to support and advance a world order broadly conducive to America's vital interests and friendly to American values, insofar as that proves feasible. In common with the slippery concept of security, order has many dimensions, including the political, the financial-economic, the environmental-ecological, and the military-strategic. In addition, world and regional order can be upset by the consequences of health crises (HIV-AIDS, most obviously), as the Spanish Flu pandemic of 1918-19 demonstrated.[104] Also, adverse climate change, uncontrolled population growth in developing countries, and increasing resource shortages—of water, food, and energy—can and most probably will incite disorder in all major dimensions of global affairs. The United States will not be equally dominant in all aspects of global order, but its policy, strategy, and actual behavior will be either regnant or at least a major player in each of those dimensions. This is what it means to be hegemonic. The world needs leadership from some sufficient source.

Although U.S. policy on global issues is often resisted, sometimes effectively, Americans nonetheless are able to help shape the global agenda and generally can exercise a potent influence on the world community's actions. Washington frequently is annoyed and frustrated by the unwillingness of others to be led by U.S. policy choices. But Americans would be far more frustrated were they either to seek to abandon the hegemonic leadership role altogether, or to resign themselves to functioning within the straitjacket of near unanimous multilateral consent. Not much would be attempted, let alone achieved, on behalf of regional and global order. American hegemonic leadership does not mean American domination. America may be dominant, indeed it will need to be dominant in its ability to persuade, bribe, and, if necessary, coerce. But it cannot guard global order by a policy of domination. Such a stance would be regarded very widely abroad as illegitimate. The predictable absence of international consent for a U.S. effort to rule by the sword, wielded by near unilateral U.S. judgment, would be fatal to the prospects for the American mission on behalf of global order. Moral authority would be absent.

2. *A national security strategy needs a named enemy.* It should remain the U.S. intention to secure its vital interests, prudently selected, and protect and perhaps advance respect for its values. But, how is this seemingly extravagant grand objective to be attempted? What does hegemonic dominance require by way of, say, economic strength (measured how? — relative size of the gross domestic product (GDP) is perhaps the usual standard, but it encourages oversimplification, e.g., ignoring size of population)? Or what does such dominance require by way of military strength, or some combination of the various elements of national power? This monograph insists upon the necessity for the United States to remain militarily ascendant in nearly all respects in most geostrategic and geopolitical contexts. But what does this mean for defense planning? To raise again a most vital question, how will future wars be fought? Where? Against whom, over what issues? And, last but not least, when? Will the American hegemon have to fight total wars of survival, which is to say wars politically and strategically comparable to

World Wars I and II and the Cold War? The truthful answer is that we do not and cannot know.

However, what we do know is that if the United States is to remain hegemonic on its own as well as on the world community's behalf, it must always be attentive to the well-being of the components of its national security strategy discussed in the immediately preceding section. Despite the title and apparent efforts of the cast of hundreds who produced it, the impressive annual document, *The National Security Strategy of the United States of America*, is more an educational endeavor than an attempt to promulgate an actual operational strategy.[105] The country cannot create a strategy to oppose terror. Terror is far too abstract, not to say diverse and dispersed, to serve as an enemy. And, to repeat, a definite strategy needs a specific, targetable enemy. The United States conducts "war planning" for many contingencies and venues, as do most states.[106]

For two centuries, powers great and small have groomed professional military and some civilian staffs, whose task is to prepare for wars of various shapes and sizes. But in order to select a dominant strategy, a country requires of its policymakers that they pick a dominant foe, at least in those cases when there is room for discretion. At present, there are several fairly plausible enemies of a still broadly hegemonic America, but, with the exception of al-Qaeda and its affiliates, none quite deserves the dubious accolade of "designated enemy of the future." On occasions, China approaches this dubious status in American perceptions. However, it is too early to be absolutely certain that China will become the dominant threat to the U.S.-led global order of the 21st century, highly probable though this development seems at present.

It follows from this analysis that U.S. national security strategy has to keep its powder dry and attuned in the face of enormous uncertainty. The scale of this uncertainty is easily illustrated by reference to the immaturity of space warfare and cyber warfare, the current debate over the relative potency of airpower and ground forces in future contingency missions, and the slow-motion strategic debates concerning the future roles of the navy and strategic nuclear forces.[107]

3. *Beware of false alternatives in policy and strategic choice.* Hegemony is a thankless lot, but it can and should offer solid as well as moral compensation. Moreover, it can work well enough to support a tolerably acceptable global order. Multipolarity will not work at all well. It would be unwelcome to Americans, and it must foster great power rivalry. Challenges to regional and global order either will not be met at all or will trigger great power conflicts. Who leads in a multipolar system? And if no state enjoys the right to lead that derives from a recognized, if resented, primacy, how are rogues and other miscreants to be contained?

American strategy does not face crisp alternatives between the conduct of irregular and regular warfare, or between an off-shore or an on-shore Eurasian continentalist military posture. It is a plain case of both/and. Often it is claimed with good reason that strategy is characterized most strongly by the need to exercise choice. With respect to U.S. military strategy in the 21st century, as in the past, the country's first strategic requirement is for competence in logistics, the science of supply and movement. Whether Americans look with most favor upon power projection by fire or by bodies, the national military strategy has to be able to direct force over trans-oceanic distances. Historical experience and common sense tell us not to draft an imaginary strategic narrative for the future out of the events of today and the recent past. This is the abominable strategic sin of "presentism." Because American military professionals cannot know today exactly what policy will require of them over the next decades, they must plan on the basis of flexibility, adaptability, historical experience, and cultural self-knowledge. They should know that there is a much preferred American way of war that is culturally founded. It favors high mobility, heavy firepower, and advanced technology. Americans should be able to recognize the moral crusader that lurks within themselves. They are ever tempted either to spread the gospel of freedom and democracy by any and all means, or to seek withdrawal from foreign entanglements when alien cultures resist American tutelage. For particular cases, America will need specific tailored strategies. Neither flexibility and adaptability, nor historical experience and cultural self-knowledge, comprise strategies.

Occasionally, very occasionally, the United States will need to engage an elusive nonstate enemy on the ground in what becomes a COIN campaign. Americans can succeed at COIN and CT, as they have demonstrated episodically for the better part of 400 years.[108] However, COIN and counterirregular warfare in general are not the American forte. It is not what the U.S. military establishment does best. Fortunately, COIN on a major scale is not asked frequently of American forces. It follows that high prowess in warfare against irregulars should not be a prominent feature in U.S. national security strategy. It would not be prudent. Almost invariably, COIN success can be achieved only within a culture by members of that culture. Americans, Britons, Frenchmen, Russians, and others are not competent to wage minimalist "war among the people," when the people at issue are culturally all but unfathomable (e.g., the NATO mission has discovered that Afghanistan contains no fewer than 60 Pushtun tribes and 400 subtribes). The United States should not choose to wage major COIN campaigns very often.[109] It will not be likely to succeed. Those Americans most probably are deluding themselves who today are predicting a largely irregular future for the country's soldiers. American culture on every level will reject the conduct of irregular warfare as the national strategic norm.

American public culture detests the moral ambiguity that inevitably attends irregular conflict. Such conflict typically is protracted, is sociologically and strategically complex, and does not usually lend itself to conclusion by decisive military action. Wars dominated by irregular tactics should therefore be avoided at almost any cost by the United States. This does not contradict the necessity for a national security strategy to develop competence in irregular warfare that leverages the value of expert military assistance on a distinctly modest scale, and a broad integrated effort to enlist help from its civilian agencies. Admittedly, the latter effort typically is frustrated by the consequences of the structure of the U.S. Government. Vietnam and Iraq do not quite constitute a pattern, but viewed together, they provide stark warning that the possibility of strategic, and hence political, failure always hovers near.

4. *Never underestimate the influence of culture.* There is an American way of war, and it persists for cultural as well as material reasons. U.S. national security strategy, as well as the policy that gives it purpose, is always going to reflect widespread national assumptions,

attitudes, preferences, and habits of behavior. Of course, American strategy must be shaped in part by realities imposed by the outside world, but perceptions of what is necessary are apt to be amazingly cultural. Political scientists enjoy debating the relative significance of the cultural and the material contexts, but the undoubted importance of the latter has to be conditioned by the former.[110] Culture is unavoidable even though Americans are not by any means prudently at liberty to pick a national strategy entirely at their own discretion. Some strategies are likely to fail if they do not suit national military prowess or the character of the threat and hence of the war. However, even when Americans are disciplined by such prominent dimensions of necessity, still they must behave as Americans, with the only cultural lens that that provides, for net good or ill in particular cases.

5. *American global leadership, or hegemony, will be challenged.* Americans must decide how hard and in which regards they will compete in order to remain Number One, but compete they must. Similarly, they need to decide how energetically they will strive to achieve a significant measure of international acquiescence in the more robust aspects of their global leadership behavior. One can hypothesize the highly unlikely event that a U.S. president could choose to eschew expensive involvement in as many global troubles as possible. He would aspire to settle for runner-up in the composite power stakes, or at best for roughly coequal multipolar player. Unfortunately, perhaps, history is not kind to strategic runners-up. The logic of global politics is at least partially zero-sum. There is an important sense in which it takes only one competitor for there to be a race for global influence and prestige. If the United States chooses not to compete energetically, others will be motivated to

race harder, not to withdraw and cease active rivalry. Those theorists are in error who speculate hopefully about the prospects for a more cooperative, gentler, kinder (than George W. Bush's) America, functioning largely multilaterally in an increasingly multipolar, but peaceable, world of consensual greater powers. No such world awaits Americans, no matter how they behave. If the country is not Number One, it will be Number Two or lower. Those who believe that that would not much matter for U.S. national security or for global order are in urgent need of a history lesson.

This analysis recommends that a sustainable American national security strategy be directed by a national security policy of leadership on behalf of global order. We should reiterate both the global need for this U.S. role, and the necessity for the substantial foreign consent vital for its successful practice. Michael Howard's 2003 caveat remains pertinent:

> American power is indispensable for the preservation of global order, and as such it must be recognized, accommodated, and where possible supported. But if it is to be effective, it needs to be seen and legitimized as such by the international community. If it is perceived rather as an instrument serving a unilateral conception of national security that amounts to a claim to world domination — pursuing, in fact a purely "American War against Terror" — that is unlikely to happen.[111]

In 2008, false perceptions of American world domination are much in abeyance as compared with 2003. The greater danger today is the possibility that the United States might retreat unduly from its role as principal guardian of what passes for global order. The years 2002-03 may be interpreted as a briefly hubristic imperial moment when, scarcely disciplined by world realities, American culture appeared to command policy and strategy. A sustainable national security strategy can be constructed only from a more modest portion of that vital ingredient.

## ENDNOTES

1. Sun-tzu, *The Art of War*, Ralph D. Sawyer, trans., Boulder, CO: Westview Press, 1994, p. 179.

2. Ross Laidlaw, *Attila: The Scourge of God*, Edinburgh: Polygon, 2007, p. 435.

3. See Hew Strachan, "The Lost Meaning of Strategy," *Survival*, Vol. 47, No. 3, Autumn 2005, pp. 33-54.

4. I will follow the convention which capitalizes International Relations as the academic discipline and employs the lower case, international relations, for the world of experience.

5. Colin Dueck, *Reluctant Crusaders: Power, Culture, and Change in American Grand Strategy*, Princeton, NJ: Princeton University Press, 2006, is a particularly fine contribution to the debate over material power versus culture. Dueck seeks with considerable success to argue a both/and position rather than a stark either/or.

6. I have written extensively about the cultural influence on U.S. policy and strategy. For recent examples, see Colin Gray: "Out of the Wilderness: Prime-time for Strategic Culture," *Comparative Strategy*, Vol. 26, No. 1, January-February 2007, pp. 1-20; and "British and American Strategic Cultures," in *Democracies in Partnership: 400 Years of Transatlantic Engagement*, The ACT/ODU Jamestown Symposium; April 18-19, 2007, Norfolk, VA: HQ, Allied Command Transformation, 2008, pp. 123-150. For a detailed and balanced review of theories of strategic culture, see Lawrence Sondhaus, *Strategic Culture and Way of War*, New York: Routledge, 2006. On the practical value of cultural study usefully nuanced for the needs of the different levels of war, see Sheila Miyoshi Jager, *On the Uses of Cultural Knowledge*, Carlisle, PA:

Strategic Studies Institute, U.S. Army War College, November 2007. For insight into the scholarly debate, see David G. Haglund, "What Good is Strategic Culture?" *International Journal*, Vol. 59, No. 3, Summer 2004, pp. 479-502.

7. It is ironic that for more than 50 years the theory of international politics in most favor among American political scientists has been one which privileges material power as the prime mover of policies everywhere. The irony lies in that the United States is one of the most ideological of countries. Nationwide values and beliefs have always either influenced or shaped American policy and strategic behavior, subject to some discipline by the more objective realities of the world. The leading school of scholars has long been known as neo-realism. The credo of this church holds that all states behave the same way regardless of their domestic differences. This nonsense was canonized in Kenneth N. Waltz, *Theory of International Politics*, Reading, MA: Addison-Wesley, 1979. There is a vast and still merrily growing academic literature on the meanings and merits of "realism" of several varieties.

8. Jeremy Black, *Great Powers and the Quest for Hegemony: The World Order since 1500*, New York: Routledge, 2008, p. 211. Black could be wrong, but I doubt it.

9. See the historical case for this judgment advanced in Donald W. Kagan, *On the Origins of War and the Preservation of Peace*, New York: Doubleday, 1995, p. 570. "What seems to work best, even though imperfectly, is the possession by those who wish to preserve the peace of the preponderant power and of the will to accept the burdens and responsibilities required to achieve that power." This view is as historically plausible as it is politically incorrect today among American scholars and commentators.

10. On the logic and significance of geopolitics and geostrategy, see Colin S. Gray, "Inescapable Geography," *The Journal of Strategic Studies*, Vol. 22, Nos. 2/3, June/September 1999, pp. 161-177.

11. See Dueck, *Reluctant Crusaders*, for a superior exposition of this argument.

12. The distinctly un-American concept of "Fighting the Long

War" was announced in Donald H. Rumsfeld, *Quadrennial Defense Review Report*, Washington, DC: U.S. Department of Defense, February 6, 2006, pp. 9-18.

13. For especially persuasive analyses of the main course of international relations in the 1920s and 1930s, see P. M. H. Bell, *The Origins of the Second World War in Europe*, 2nd Ed., London: Longman, 1997; and Jeffrey Record, *The Specter of Munich: Reconsidering the Lessons of Appeasing Hitler*, Washington, DC: Potomac Books, 2007.

14. For the fundamental geopolitical logic behind U.S. policy, see Halford J. Mackinder, *Democratic Ideals and Reality*, New York: Norton 1962. The title study was written and first published in 1919, while the key paper, reprinted in the book, "The Geographical Pivot of History," dates to 1904. An intriguing geopolitical perspective on American foreign policy is C. Dale Walton, *Geopolitics and the Great Powers in the Twenty-First Century: Multipolarity and the Revolution in Strategic Perspective*, New York: Routledge, 2007. The enduring importance of geography for statecraft is well argued through historical cases in Jakub J. Grygiel, *Great Powers and Geopolitical Change*, Baltimore: The Johns Hopkins University Press, 2006.

15. Christopher Layne, "Impotent Power? Reexamining the Nature of America's Hegemonic Power," *The National Interest*, No. 85, September/October 2006, p. 47.

16. Abstract and "big picture" master narratives have difficulty giving due regard to historical detail. Rational actor theory simply assumes away, or just ignores, accidents, human eccentricities and folly, and the consequences of the fog of peace and war that obliges policymakers to perform while in a condition of notable ignorance. The concept of the fog of war is pure Clausewitz; see *On War*, Michael Howard and Peter Paret, trans., Princeton, NJ: Princeton University Press, 1976, p. 140. "Finally, the general unreliability of all information presents a special problem in war: all action takes place, so to speak, in a kind of twilight, which, like fog or moonlight, often tends to make things seem grotesque and larger than they really are." On the fog of peace and its implications for planners, see Talbot C. Imlay and Marcia Duffy Toft, eds., *The Fog of Peace and War Planning: Military and Strategic Planning under Uncertainty*, New York: Routledge, 2006.

17. See Clausewitz, pp. 177-183, 607.

18. Harry R. Yarger, *Strategic Theory for the 21st Century: The Little Book on Big Strategy*, Carlisle, PA: Strategic Studies Institute, U.S. Army War College, February 2006, is strong on the fundamentals.

19. Michael Howard, "British Grand Strategy in World War I," in Paul Kennedy, ed., *Grand Strategies in War and Peace*, New Haven, CT: Yale University Press, 1991, p. 32.

20. Lord Kitchener commenting on the British military situation in 1915, quoted in Michael Howard, *The Continental Commitment: The Dilemma of British Defence Policy in the Era of the Two World Wars*, London: Temple Smith, 1972, p. 126.

21. See Colin S. Gray, *Irregular Enemies and the Essence of Strategy: Can the American Way of War Adapt?* Carlisle, PA: Strategic Studies Institute, U.S. Army War College, March 2006.

22. I defend and explain this controversial claim in "The American Way of War: Critique and Implications," in Anthony D. Mc Ivor, ed., *Rethinking the Principles of War*, Annapolis, MD: *Naval Institute Proceedings*, 2005, pp. 13-40.

23. As a country blessed with exceptionally bountiful resources and an enviable geopolitical context, the United States has enjoyed a great deal of discretion over its national security policy and strategy. It would be needless to add that the country did not grow from being 13 very divided colonies clinging to the Eastern seaboard, to a continental size super-state, by humility and turning the other cheek.

24. See Geoffrey Perret, *A Country Made by War: From the Revolution to Vietnam — the Story of America's Rise to Power*, New York: Vintage Books, 1989; and Jeremy Black, *America as a Military Power: From the American Revolution to the Civil War*, Westport, CT: Praeger Publishers, 2002.

25. On America as "globocop," see Colin S. Gray, *The Sheriff: America's Defense of the New World Order*, Lexington: The University

70

Press of Kentucky, 2004. Although I believe the basic argument of this book to be sound, I should have placed more emphasis upon the American ideological impulse to remake benighted lands. I am grateful to Andrew J. Bacevich for his criticism in this regard. Bacevich, a retired army officer, has been skeptical of America's ability to govern its informal empire, its imperium. See his *American Empire: The Realities and Consequences of U.S. Diplomacy*, Cambridge, MA: Harvard University Press, 2002; and *The New American Militarism: How Americans are Seduced by War*, Oxford: Oxford University Press, 2005. Although they are highly critical of contemporary policy and strategy, these books are far from hysterical in tone. They are moderate statements of well-reasoned points of view.

26. See Henry Kissinger: *A World Restored: Europe after Napoleon: The Politics of Conservatism in a Revolutionary Age*, New York: Grosset and Dunlop, 1964; and *Diplomacy*, New York: Simon and Schuster, 1994.

27. For leading period pieces, see Charles Krauthammer, "The Unipolar Moment," *Foreign Affairs*, Vol. 70, No. 1, 1990-1991, pp. 23-34; *idem.*, "The Unipolar Moment Revisited," *The National Interest*, No. 70, Winter 2002-2003, pp. 5-17. For a skeptical view of the probable longevity of America's "unipolar moment," see Christopher Layne, *The Peace of Illusions: American Grand Strategy from 1940 to the Present*, Ithaca, NY: Cornell University Press, 2006, Ch. 7.

28. The principal sign of the times concerning semi-organized efforts to balance the United States is the creation of the Shanghai Cooperation Organization (SCO). The SCO's current membership comprises the Russian Federation, China, Tajikistan, Kyrgyzstan, Kazakhstan, and Uzbekistan. These states held well-advertised joint military exercises in August 2007. Contrary to alarmist Western newspaper reports, the SCO is many major steps distant from constituting a "rival to NATO." (Tony Halpin, "Rival to NATO Begins First Military Exercise," *The Times* [London], August 6, 2006, p. 32.) However, the very existence of the SCO and its ability to attract "observers" and "associates" from other countries unfriendly towards the United States does warrant serious notice as a possible historical marker.

29. For a distinctly superior example of the critical genre, see Bacevich, *The New American Militarism.*

30. See Black, *Great Powers and the Quest for Hegemony*, p. 237.

31. Eliot A. Cohen, *Supreme Command: Soldiers, Statesmen, and Leadership in Wartime*, New York: The Free Press, 2002.

32. "Soldiers" refers generically to military professionals. I apologize for any offense that this expedient usage this may cause among sailors and airmen, not to mention spacemen and cybermen, or among female service personnel.

33. Dueck, *Reluctant Crusaders*, Ch. 1, provides a persuasive theoretical treatment of the concept of grand strategy.

34. See David A. Baldwin, "Security Studies and the End of the Cold War," *World Politics*, Vol. 48, No. 1, October 1995, pp. 117-141; and Richard K. Betts, "Should Strategic Studies Survive?" *World Politics*, Vol. 50, No. 1, October 1997, pp. 7-33.

35. Clausewitz, esp. p. 127.

36. Bernard B. Fall, *Street Without Joy*, New York: Schocken Books, 1972, p. 375. I am grateful to Stephen J. Cimbala, one of whose publications reminded me of the value of Fall's thought, as quoted.

37. Bernard Fall, *Hell in a Very Small Place: The Siege of Dien Bien Phu*, New York: Da Capo, 1985, esp. pp. 450, 479-482; and Martin Windrow, *The Last Valley: Dien Bien Phu and the French Defeat in Vietnam*, London: Weidenfeld and Nicolson, 2004, are excellent.

38. See Martin S. Alexander and J. F. Keiger, eds., *France and the Algerian War, 1954-62: Strategy, Operations and Diplomacy*, London: Frank Cass, 2002, esp. pp. 701-703.

39. I discuss the crucial relationship between fighting and war's outcome in my *Fighting Talk: Forty Maxims on War, Peace, and Strategy*, Westport, CT: Praeger Security International, 2007, pp. 32-35, 105-108.

40. This is not to argue that Germany could not have defeated the Soviet Union. But it is to suggest that there were limitations in the German way of war which are attributable to strategic and military cultural biases rather than to bad luck or geography. Robert M. Citino, *The German Way of War: From the Thirty Years' War to the Third Reich*, Lawrence, KS: University Press of Kansas, 2005; idem., *Blitzkrieg to Desert Storm: The Evolution of Operational Warfare*, Lawrence, KS: University Press of Kansas, 2004, Ch. 2, are persuasive. The German way of war favored rapid operational maneuver in short, militarily decisive campaigns. Intelligence, logistics, and strategy were never its strong points.

41. See "Briefing: Iraq and Afghanistan," *The Economist*, December 15, 2007, pp. 31-36, for a balanced assessment of the recent COIN performance of the U.S. Army.

42. Clausewitz, pp. 85-86, 104, 119-123.

43. *Ibid.*, pp. 101, 86, respectively.

44. Terence M. Holmes, "Planning versus Chaos in Clausewitz's *On War*," *The Journal of Strategic Studies*, Vol. 30, No. 1, February 2007, pp. 129-151, provides a most useful corrective to the standard view, which typically neglects to notice that Clausewitz, although stressing uncertainty and chance, also endorsed planning and strategy.

45. Clausewitz, Book Eight.

46. *Ibid.*, Book One, Ch. 3. Also see the brief discussion of genius in *On War* in Hew Strachan, *Clausewitz's On War: A Biography*, New York: Atlantic Monthly Press, 2007, pp. 94-96, 127-129.

47. It is no exaggeration to claim that from the late 1950s until the end of the Cold War, the so-called uncertainty principle lay at the heart of U.S. nuclear strategy. In the face of an undeniable incredibility over the promise to take action that would amount to national suicide, the United States signed on at the highest level for Thomas C. Schelling's concept of "the threat that leaves something to chance." This dangerous and dubious idea squared the circle for American policymakers. Such threats enabled the United States to expand nuclear deterrence to protect distant

friends and allies, at least so it was argued by American officials for more than 30 years: this strange idea was (un)holy writ. See Thomas C. Schelling, *The Strategy of Conflict*, New York: Galaxy, 1963, Ch. 8, "The Threat That Leaves Something to Chance."

48. On the challenge of uncertainty for defense planners, see Michael Fitzsimmons, "The Problems of Uncertainty in Strategic Planning," *Survival*, Vol. 48, No. 4, Winter 2006-07, pp. 131-146; and Colin S. Gray, "Coping with Uncertainty: Dilemmas of Defence Planning," *The British Army Review*, No. 143, Autumn 2007, pp. 36-40.

49. For example, see Holmes, "Planning versus Chaos in Clausewitz's *On War*."

50. See Richard K. Betts, "Is Strategy an Illusion?" *International Security*, Vol. 25, No. 2, Fall 2000, pp. 5-50.

51. Paul M. Kennedy, ed., *The War Plans of the Great Powers, 1880-1914*, London: George Allen and Unwin, 1979. Careful studies that focus on planning by just one or two states include: John Gooch, *The Plans of War: The General Staff and British Military Strategy, c.1900-1916*, London: Routledge and Kegan Paul, 1974; Arden Bucholz, *Moltke, Schlieffen, and Prussian War Planning*, New York, Berg, 1991; Graydon A. Tunstall, Jr., *Planning for War Against Russia and Serbia: Austro-Hungarian and German Military Strategies, 1871-1941*, Highland Lakes, NJ: Atlantic Research and Publications, 1993; and Steven T. Ross, *American War Plans, 1945-1950*, London: Frank Cass, 1996.

52. Imlay and Toft, eds., *The Fog of Peace and War Planning*.

53. Marcia Toft and Talbot Imlay, "Strategic and Military Planning under the Fog of Peace," *ibid.*, pp. 1-2.

54. I recall Herman Kahn recounting how he attempted to make this important point to a congressional committee, only to find that the members resisted the logic. They did not want to believe him.

55. As in Colin S. Gray, *Another Bloody Century: Future Warfare*, London: Weidenfeld and Nicolson, 2005. With justice friendly

critics have pointed out that in this book I both issue warnings about, even against, the perils of prediction, and then proceed to predict anyway.

56. A global communitarianism vision is one such radical alternative. See Amitai Etzioni, *From Empire to Community: A New Approach to International Relations*, Basingstoke, UK: Palgrave Macmillan, 2004. For a skeptical assessment, see Colin S. Gray, "Sandcastle of Theory: A Critique of Amitai Etzioni's Communitarianism," *American Behavioral Scientist*, Vol. 48, No. 12, August 2005, pp. 1607-1625.

57. See Robert E. Harkavy, *Strategic Basing and the Great Powers, 1200-2000*, New York: Routledge, 2007, esp. Ch. 7, "After the Cold War: basing in a unipolar system." No one can accuse Harkavy of lacking historical range.

58. The "new wars" literature includes the following works: Martin van Creveld, *The Transformation of War*, New York: The Free Press, 1991; Chris Hables Gray, *Postmodern War: The New Politics of Conflict*, London: Routledge, 1997; Mary Kaldor, *New and Old Wars: Organized Violence in a Global Era*, Cambridge: Polity Press, 1999; Christopher Coker, *Future War: The Re-Enchantment of War in the Twenty-First Century*, Oxford: Blackwell Publishing, 2004; Herfried Münkler, *The New Wars*, Cambridge: Polity Press, 2005; Isabelle Duyvesteyn and Jan Angstrom, eds., *Rethinking the Nature of War*, New York: Frank Cass, 2005; and Rupert Smith, *The Utility of Force: The Art of War in the Modern World*, London: Allen Lane, 2005. The view that major interstate war is now obsolete is argued in Michael Mandelbaum, "Is Major War Obsolete?" *Survival*, Vol. 40, No. 4, Winter 1998-99, pp. 20-38. For an interesting if over-ambitious attempt to unravel "the riddle of war," see Azar Gat, *War in Human Civilization*, Oxford: Oxford University Press, 2006. Readers should find value also in David J. Lonsdale, *The Nature of War in the Information Age: Clausewitzian Future*, New York: Frank Cass, 2004.

59. Technology plays a prominent role in the following useful analyses: Benjamin S. Lambeth, *The Transformation of American Air Power*, Ithaca, NY: Cornell University Press, 2000; Mc Ivor, ed., *Rethinking the Principles of War*; Frederick W. Kagan, *Finding the Target: The Transformation of American Military Policy*, New York: Encounter Books, 2006; Max Boot, *War Made New: Technology,*

*Warfare, and the Course of History, 1500 to Today*, New York: Gotham Books, 2006; and Martin van Creveld, *The Changing Face of War: Lessons of Combat from the Marne to Iraq*, New York: Ballantine Books, 2006.

60. See Colin S. Gray, "Technology as a Dynamic of Defence Transformation," *Defence Studies*, Vol. 6, No. 1, March 2006, pp. 26-51.

61. Clausewitz, p. 606.

62. The concept of "disruptive technology" warrants more attention than it has received to date. As a pioneering historical study, Terry C. Pierce, *Warfighting and Disruptive Technology: Disguising Innovation*, New York: Frank Cass, 2004, is highly recommended.

63. Walton, *Geopolitics and the Great Powers in the Twenty-first Century*, pp. 105-106.

64. *Ibid.*, p. 106.

65. It can be helpful to think of order as coming in world, regional, and local, varieties. Although order generally is favored as an often presumed prerequisite for security, the concept is not bereft of sinister associations. Recall "The New Order" introduced as and by the Third Reich. It would be agreeable to employ the concept only in a value-free descriptive sense, but alas that is not possible. The idea of order is employed descriptively, prescriptively, and normatively, whether or not scholars approve of the confusion that such intellectual indiscipline cannot help promoting. From a large body of writings, theoretical and historical, see Hedley Bull, *The Anarchical Society – A Study of Order in World Politics*, New York: Columbia University Press, 1977; Anja V. Hartmann and Beatrice Heuser, eds., *War, Peace and World Order in European History*, New York: Routledge, 2001; and G. John Ikenberry, *After Victory: Institutions, Strategic Restraint, and the Rebuilding of Order After Major Wars*, Princeton, NJ: Princeton University Press, 2001.

66. Clausewitz, p. 97.

67. In World War II U.S. military mobilization favored the U.S. Army Air Forces and the U.S. Navy over the U.S. Army. To illustrate: in effect the Navy had no force structure goals to meet, it simply grew to be as large as the shipyards permitted, literally regardless of manning problems. In contrast, the Wehrmacht was always geared to maximize its ground power, both in quantity and quality. See Max Hastings, *Nemesis: The Battle for Japan, 1944-45*, London Harper Press, 2007, Ch. 4. ". . . with Pearl Harbor to be avenged, there was no political will to challenge the ambitions of the U.S. Navy," p. 103. Although he is an accomplished and well-regarded popular historian in Britain, it is well to remember that Sir Max is not known for generous judgments on Americans.

68. See Roger W. Barnett, *Asymmetrical Warfare: Today's Challenge to U.S. Military Power*, Washington, DC: Brassey's, 2003.

69. The idea of a cultural assumption is well explained in Jeremy Black, *Rethinking Military History*, New York: Routledge, 2004, pp. 13-22.

70. It is helpful to recall that World War II comprised two gigantic siege operations, continental in and for Europe and maritime for East Asia. The key reasons for the geostrategic differences between the two wars are scarcely less significant in the 21st century than they were in the mid-20th.

71. Walton, *Geopolitics and the Great Powers in the Twenty-first Century*, p. 43.

72. There is persisting merit in Aaron L. Friedberg, "Will Europe's Past be Asia's Future?" *Survival*, Vol. 42, No. 3, Autumn 2000, pp. 147-159.

73. The *Quadrennial Defense Review Report* of 2006 described how the Department of Defense was shifting its emphasis "from a time of reasonable predictability—to an era of surprise and uncertainty." Rumsfeld, *Quadrennial Defense Review Report*, p. vi. But see Fitzsimmons, "The Problem of Uncertainty in Strategic Planning," for a strongly mounted critique of the uncertainty principle. It is the opinion of this author that although Fitzsimmons scores some points, in general his critical argument overreaches.

74. Walton, *Geopolitics and the Great Powers in the Twenty-first Century*, pp. 105-106, opens an intriguing vista of a dynamic and technologically advanced future for warfare.

75. See Michael I. Handel, "Intelligence and the Problem of Strategic Surprise," and James J. Wirtz, "Theory of Surprise," in Richard K. Betts and Thomas C. Mahnken, eds., *Paradoxes of Strategic Intelligence: Essays in Honor of Michael I. Handel*, London: Frank Cass, 2003, pp. 1-58, 100-116; and Colin S. Gray, *Transformation and Strategic Surprise*, Carlisle, PA: Strategic Studies Institute, U.S. Army War College, April 2005.

76. Justin Wintle, ed., *The Dictionary of War Quotations*, New York: The Free Press, 1989, p. 377.

77. Bush, *National Security Strategy of the United States of America*, September 2002, p. 1 (emphasis added).

78. *Ibid.*

79. *Ibid.*, p. i.

80. Morton Halperin, "Nuclear Weapons and Limited War," *The Journal of Conflict Resolution*, Vol. V, No. 2, June 1961, p. 161.

81. I analyze the slippery concept of policy in *Strategic Studies and Public Policy: The American Experience*, Lexington, KY: The University Press of Kentucky, Ch. 2.

82. Thucydides, *The Landmark Thucydides: A Comprehensive Guide to The Peloponnesian War*, Robert B. Strassler, ed., New York: The Free Press, 1996, p. 43.

83. Black, *Rethinking Military History*, pp. 13-22, is exceptionally perceptive on the relationship between public and strategic cultures.

84. Barry R. Posen, "Command of the Commons: The Military Foundation of U.S. Hegemony," *International Security*, Vol. 28, No. 1, Summer 2003, pp. 5-46. Also see Barry R. Posen, "Exit Strategy: How to disengage from Iraq in 18 months," *Boston Review*, January/February 2006, accessed on December 2, 2007, at *bostonreview.net/BR31.1/posen.html*.

85. Layne, *The Peace of Illusions*, advances this as his preferred policy option.

86. J. C. Wylie, *Military Strategy: A General Theory of Power Control*, Annapolis, MD: Naval Institute Press, 1989, p. 72 (emphasis added).

87. Unfortunately, President Bush was not correct when in 2006 he claimed that "[t]he great struggles of the 20th century between liberty and totalitarianism ended with a decisive victory for the forces of freedom. . . ." *The National Security Strategy of the United States of America*, p. i. "Victory," yes, but "decisive," alas not yet.

88. The "imperial overstretch" thesis was advanced as the master narrative in Paul Kennedy, *The Rise and Fall of the Great Powers: Economic Change and Military Conflict from 1500 to 2000*, New York: Random House, 1987.

89. The valid reason for the American-led invasion in 2003 was to demonstrate that states cannot defy the laws and norms of the nascent world community and its own supposedly solemn international obligations, and escape corrective action and punishment. For more than a decade, Saddam Hussein's regime defied that community and, in effect, challenged it to do its worst. The proper rationale for the 2003 invasion was the enforcement of international law and norms, not the issue of WMD or possible connections between Baghdad and al-Qaeda. American national culture most probably would have supported President Bush had he chosen to emphasize the enforcement of right conduct and the correction of roguish behavior. There was no need to manufacture, or certainly exaggerate, other less abstract rationales.

90. Jeremy Black argues plausibly that "[p]owerful states expect to dominate their neighbours and do not appreciate opposition to this aspiration, as Russia has demonstrated in the Caucasus in the 1990s and 2000s—for example, in its aggressive policy towards Georgia." *Great Powers and the Quest for Hegemony*, p. 231.

91. The most vital principle underpinning "Concert" diplomacy was the informal rule that no great power would behave in a manner potentially detrimental to the interests of another great power, without first consulting that other power. A process of consultation, even a habit of such, would enable the great powers to avoid needless conflict among themselves. This "system" was never robust, but it did have some substance to it until the 1850s. Furthermore, it can be argued that the memory of a great power Concert, even if it had become a lost habit, did give evidence of life in the late 1870s with the Congress of Berlin, and limped into the 1900s, albeit unverified by actual behavior. Certainly the great power Concert of the first half of the 19th century, such as it was, and admittedly it did not amount to much, was a definite precursor to the Council of the League of Nations, the United Nations Security Council, and even today's G-8. Each of these institutions was designed to function as a great power club. A relatively positive view of the 19th century Congress and Concert systems is advanced in Paul W. Schroeder, *The Transformation of European Politics, 1763-1848*, Oxford: The Clarendon Press, 1994.

92. For a stimulating discussion of errors and learning in war, see Victor Davis Hanson, "In War, Resolution," *Claremont Review of Books*, Vol. VIII, No. 1, Winter 2007/08, pp. 8-12. The now almost classic study is Eliot A. Cohen and John Gooch, *Military Misfortunes: The Anatomy of Failure in War*, New York: The Free Press, 1990, which would merit the overemployed description as brilliant had it taken "the enemy" more seriously.

93. See Posen, "Command of the Commons."

94. See John Arquilla and David Ronfeldt, eds., *In Athena's Camp: Preparing for Conflict in the Information Age*, Santa Monica, CA: RAND, 1997; Alan D. Campen and Douglas H. Dearth, eds., *Cyberwar 3.0:Human Factors in Information Operations and Future Conflict*, Fairfax, VA: AFCEA International Press, 2000; Bruce Berkowitz, *The New Face of War: How War Will Be Fought in the 21st Century*, New York: The Free Press, 2003; Wayne Michael Hall, *Stray Voltage: War in the Information Age*, Annapolis, MD: Naval Institute Press, 2003; and especially Lonsdale, *The Nature of War in the Information Age*.

95. Julian S. Corbett, *Some Principles of Maritime Strategy, 1911*, Annapolis, MD: Naval Institute Press, 1988, p. 16.

96. Imlay and Toft, eds., *The Fog of Peace and War Planning*.

97. Smith, *The Utility of Force*.

98. We cannot be at all sure that interstate war is obsolete, indeed even major interstate wars may occur. Such is the view expressed in Gray, *Another Bloody Century*. For a fundamentally different perspective, that from the doyen of theorists of "critical security studies," see Ken Booth, *Theory of World Security*, Cambridge, MA: Cambridge University Press, 2007, pp. 225 ff.

99. Kennedy, *The Rise and Fall of the Great Powers*.

100. This important point is made strongly in Black, *Great Powers and the Quest for Hegemony*, p. 234.

101. Richard K. Betts, "The Trouble with Strategy: Bridging Policy and Operations," *Joint Force Quarterly*, No. 29, Autumn/Winter 2001-02, pp. 23-30, characerically is useful.

102. The now classic statement of the American ideal is Samuel P. Huntington, *The Soldier and the State: The Theory and Politics of Civil-Military Relations*, New York: Vintage Books, 1964.

103. But Clausewitz is where one should begin. He does warn, famously, that "[e]verything in strategy is very simple, but that does not mean that everything is very easy." p. 178.

104. See John Barry, *The Great Influenza: The Epic Story of the Deadliest Plague in History*, London: Penguin Books, 2005.

105. Norman Friedman, "The Real Purpose of Strategy," *U.S. Naval Institute Proceedings*, Vol. 133, No. 12, December 2007, pp. 90-91, is to the point.

106. Other favored high concepts include "strategic planning" and "policy planning." For an insightful and constructive recent critique of deficiencies in the machinery for such U.S. planning, see Aaron L. Friedberg, "Strengthening U.S. Strategic Planning,"

*The Washington Quarterly*, Vol. 31, No. 1, Winter 2007-08, pp. 47-60.

107. A window into one important room in the current house of debate is David E. Johnson, *Learning Large Lessons: The Evolving Roles of Ground Power and Air Power in the Post-Cold War Era*, Santa Monica, CA: RAND, 2006.

108. One might observe that the U.S. colonial conduct of irregular warfare against native Americans certainly was ultimately effective. However, typically it was neither elegant nor did it manifest what today is regarded as best practice in COIN. Power and persistence usually triumph if they are sufficiently ruthless, overwhelming, and protracted. The nearly 400 years of warfare on its internal frontier was always going to conclude with a decisive victory for the mightiest, albeit intruding, belligerent. Natural justice does not ensure that strategic history is a morality tale, while one should not be unduly in thrall to the legend of the "noble savage."

109. Unfortunately, this central issue is not addressed in Jager, *On the Uses of Cultural Knowledge*. Professor Jager writes persuasively of the value of this knowledge. So much is not really at issue. But she proceeds to the next step, on applicability, and overreaches when she advises that "a sound strategic framework based on a deep cultural and historical understanding of an adversary culture will necessarily give rise to sound operations and tactics necessary for waging a successful counterinsurgency," p. 4. Jager's "necessarily" is, alas, too strong. Nothing can guarantee the adoption, let alone the actual exercise, of "sound operations and tactics," though cultural empathy for a local society certainly should help, it can hardly hinder. Cultural understanding, even when it is truly "deep," is not a panacea for America's COIN challenges. Moreover, while it meets a clear instrumental need, it will not meet a political one unless the analysis strives specifically to do so. Jager's well informed work points usefully to the need for cultural study to "redefine an overarching strategic framework for counterinsurgency," but we need to consider the cultural dimension at a yet higher level as well. Should the United States be pursuing purposes that oblige it to adopt a strategy that entails fighting in the midst of foreign societies?